How to Be
Abby

How to Be Abby

A Cat's Guide to Happiness

Henry Grbac

ARCHWAY PUBLISHING

Copyright © 2022 Henry Grbac.

All rights reserved. No part of this book may be used or reproduced by any means, graphic, electronic, or mechanical, including photocopying, recording, taping or by any information storage retrieval system without the written permission of the author except in the case of brief quotations embodied in critical articles and reviews.

This book is a work of non-fiction. Unless otherwise noted, the author and the publisher make no explicit guarantees as to the accuracy of the information contained in this book and in some cases, names of people and places have been altered to protect their privacy.

Archway Publishing books may be ordered through booksellers or by contacting:

Archway Publishing
1663 Liberty Drive
Bloomington, IN 47403
www.archwaypublishing.com
844-669-3957

Because of the dynamic nature of the Internet, any web addresses or links contained in this book may have changed since publication and may no longer be valid. The views expressed in this work are solely those of the author and do not necessarily reflect the views of the publisher, and the publisher hereby disclaims any responsibility for them.

Any people depicted in stock imagery provided by Getty Images are models, and such images are being used for illustrative purposes only. Certain stock imagery © Getty Images.

Scripture taken from the Holy Bible, NEW INTERNATIONAL VERSION®. Copyright © 1973, 1978, 1984, 2011 by Biblica, Inc. All rights reserved worldwide. Used by permission. NEW INTERNATIONAL VERSION® and NIV® are registered trademarks of Biblica, Inc. Use of either trademark for the offering of goods or services requires the prior written consent of Biblica US, Inc.

ISBN: 978-1-6657-2102-8 (sc)
ISBN: 978-1-6657-2100-4 (hc)
ISBN: 978-1-6657-2101-1 (e)

Library of Congress Control Number: 2022905722

Print information available on the last page.

Archway Publishing rev. date: 4/27/2022

To my wife, Joanne; my daughter, Jessica; and my cat, Abby

CONTENTS

Preface	**xi**
Introduction: Who Is Abby	**xiii**
How to Be Happy	xv
The Definition of Happiness	xvi
Spoiler Alert	xvii
Back to Happiness	xix
Learning to Take a Nap	xxi
Chapter 1: The Journey	**1**
Finding Your Tranquility	3
The Tool of Forgiving	8
Letting Go of the Story. The Ego	14
Chapter 2: Dealing with Unpleasantry to Get Back to Clarity and Peace	**21**
Learning Mindfulness and Meditation	23
Mindfulness	23
How Does Meditation Help? What Is the Connection to Mindfulness?	26
Meditation Practice	27

Body Scan Meditation	30
Listening Meditation	33
Walking Meditation	35
Compassion and Kindness for Yourself	36
Using Compassion and Kindness to Deal with Unpleasantry	38
Tapping into and Creating an Abundance of Compassion and Kindness	40

Chapter 3: Even Abby Can Get Frustrated — 42
The Coffee Mug	47
Letting-Go Coconut Meditation	50
Dealing with Unpleasantry, Such as Frustration	51
Sensory Awareness Meditation (SAM)	53

Chapter 4: Nourishing Happiness — 56
Tools to Nourish Happiness	59

Chapter 5: We Need to Be Kind to Ourselves Because It Is Not Entirely Our Fault — 71
Ways to be Kind to Yourself	75
Summary	83

Chapter 6: Spiritual Wellness and Happiness — 85
Spiritual Being	89
How Aware Are You of Your Self? Reflection	91
Greater Awareness of Ourselves through Prayer	94
Three Steps to Help You with Self-Change	96

Chapter 7: Happiness Teachings   **104**
    Jesus Christ—The Sermon on the Mount   106
    The Buddha—The Four Noble Truths and the
       Noble Eightfold Path   113

Chapter 8: Pain and Suffering—
The Teacher of Happiness   **121**
    Pain and Suffering—Empathy to Happiness   134
    Having a Bad Day? Receive Some
       Compassion, Comfort and Love Meditation   138

Chapter 9: Are You Walking the Path of
Happiness?   **140**

Chapter 10: Finding Goals and a Life Purpose   **155**
    Goals   162
    Courage   164
    Self-Doubt, Insecurities, Lack of Confidence   167
    Summary   170
    Finding Your Purpose in Life Guide   171

Chapter 11: A Short Story—
"The Enlightened Cat"   **174**

Closing Meows   **195**

PREFACE

I HAVE A CAT NAMED ABBY. IT SOUNDS SILLY, BUT SHE HAS MANY life examples in what it means to be happy. *How to Be Abby: A Cat's Guide to Happiness* is a book to help you connect to happiness. It will teach you how to respond appropriately to life's unpleasantries to avoid suffering and reach states of peace.

Learn how to use mindfulness, meditation, self-compassion, and loving-kindness to experience a complete life that is already within you. Acquire a variety of tools to nourish your happiness. Learn what it means to be kind to yourself to inspire self-acceptance, regardless of who you are. Explore spiritual wellness to understand spiritual connection to happiness. Discover other happiness teachings from the Sermon on the Mount and the Four Noble Truths. Find the answer to the question, how does pain and suffering lead to happiness? And finally, apply all the teachings to help you find your goals in life and your life purpose.

Both Abby and I wish you a successful journey in your guide to happiness.

INTRODUCTION

Who Is Abby?

ABBY IS MY CAT, OF COURSE. SHE IS A CALICO, AND MY FAMILY AND I have had her for over seventeen years, and she still amazes me. Just the other day, I caught her sleeping with her tongue out. How cute is that? She brings so much joy and happiness to our lives, even though she sleeps twenty hours a day. And when she sleeps, it's so peaceful just to look at her. A cat that has been with us for over seventeen years is no longer a cat but a family member. We treat her as if she's one of our own kids. My daughter would argue that a cat looks upon its owners as its own kittens. So now I wonder—who's taking care of whom?

Recently, she has started to limp, as she has some arthritis in her leg. A seventeen-year-old cat is eighty-four in human age. I don't want to think about it, and I try not to think about it, but I know that one day she won't be with us. With this in mind, I try to cherish each day and each moment with my lovable cat. I read somewhere that the name *Abigail*—or Abby, for short—means happy or joyful. And this is why I chose the title to this book: *How to Be Abby: A Cat's Guide to Happiness.* So let's begin to our guide to happiness!

I like being happy; who doesn't? I love taking long walks with my wife and daughter. Walking on a trail surrounded by trees and nature is so calming and relaxing. On the flip side, I also like shopping. Buying stuff or even dreaming of buying stuff that I can't afford is somewhat hypnotic. I think about what kind of stuff I would buy if I won millions of dollars. A sports car? A cottage on the lake? A new house with all the latest bells and whistles? Or how about a house in the Caribbean? So many things to think about. My wife and I love watching TV shows that center upon buying homes somewhere exotic, where it's warm and near the sea. So nice to dream and think about all the possibilities.

But wait a second! This book is about Abby. Abby doesn't live in the Caribbean or drive a fast car or go shopping. She sleeps most of the day. She pretty much eats the same food, day after day, with some exceptions of my sneaking in some unhealthy human food to her—my daughter blames me for Abby being overweight. The things that make Abby happy are sitting outside and eating grass, then puking shortly afterward. She loves to sit in the sun and scratch herself on anything that is made of concrete.

And the one thing that makes her happy (I say this because she purrs forever) is to sit in our laps while we watch TV. How simple is that? My wife says that she would love to be reincarnated as a cat. Is there a connection to being happy and being a cat? OK, Abby. What are your secrets to being happy? Nope. No answer from Abby. All I get is a lot of purring and wanting me to pet her. It's time to see what Google says about how to be happy.

How to Be Happy

When we Google "how to be happy," we get a lot of information. We get "25 Tips to Be Happy," "15 Scientifically Proven Ways to Be Happy," all sorts of videos, many great books, and even quizzes and tests that we can take to see how happy we are. The information is phenomenal. I can't believe the wealth of information available on how to be happy.

I know I want to be happy, but I'm not sure how to get there. When I read through some of these tips and ways to be happy, it all seemed like good advice. I even tried some of the quizzes or tests that give a "happy index" score on how happy you are. Generally speaking, the quizzes said that I'm doing OK.

The one thing that I realized from this information is that if you want to be happy, then you need to put effort into being happy. But when I look at Abby, I don't see her putting effort into trying to be happy. She just seems to be happy overall. She's not doing anything when she's sitting on my lap, but I know she's happy because she's purring. She's not doing anything when she's sitting in the sun, scratching herself on the concrete, yet I know she's happy because she's purring. So I'm confused right now if you need to put effort into being happy—or not.

Guess the next question to ask myself is, what's the difference between trying to be happy—or, more precisely, doing things to be happy—and simply being in the state of happiness? Is there a connection between doing and not doing to get happiness? The one thing I do know is that these questions are not making me happy. If anything, I'm making myself more confused and frustrated because there seem to be more questions than answers.

So what do I do now? I think I need to find the definition of *happiness*.

The Definition of Happiness

If I look at Abby, I would define happiness as simply being at peace, being calm, and being in the present moment. Abby is very peaceful; hence, this is why I say *being at peace*. Abby is very calm—unless she's asking for unhealthy human food, but overall, very calm. And I would argue that Abby lives in the present moment. How do I know this? That is a fair question. To answer, I'm going to ask Abby if she lives in the present moment. Nope. No answer. Just a lot of purring.

I've read a lot of books that say you need to be and to live in the present moment to be happy. That makes sense to me and to Abby. But even a cat can't be happy all the time. When Abby is limping because of her arthritis, I'm sure she is experiencing some discomfort. When I've injured myself, besides the physical pain there is also the mental anguish that comes with it. I think, *Is this pain ever going to go away? How long will it take for my body to heal? What happens if this becomes a permanent injury?* My mind keeps generating thought after thought. During these times, it's difficult to be happy or to be at peace. Many phrases describe these situations: Life is like hills and valleys, ups and downs. Life is like a garden. Life is like a bowl of spaghetti. Have you heard this one? "Life is like Abby; you are either sleeping or sleeping." For me, most of these phrases, including the one that I just made up, don't seem to help me much when I'm on a hill or in a valley. There must be something more to help our happiness.

Spoiler Alert

I've been doing meditation for over twelve years now. I was not introduced to this topic freely; instead, it found me. Let me explain: when I was in my early forties, I experienced trouble sleeping due to work and life stresses. The stress was from my inability to let go of worry. The stress that plagues me today is my inability to stay in the present moment. I think of what used to be and what should be, and because of it, I get torn, and I create stress for myself.

This stress created problems in my life, such as sleep disturbances. It's a scary thing when you can't sleep at night. And that scared me enough to realize that I needed to change my thinking patterns and how I reacted to life's situations. I started reading self-help books, and I discovered one specific tool that seemed to open a path for me to less suffering. Nobody wants to suffer, and we all want to be happy. So I started to explore this tool of meditation and how I could apply it to my life and to my overall well-being.

The word *meditation* in Western culture is still not completely accepted. For me, that is troubling because I see this tool as something that can help you and me and the rest of the world. My wife and I introduced meditation into our lives and even into our daughter's. She was around five years old when we introduced children's meditations. And our experience has been that it helped her (and still does) to deal with strong emotions.

I do understand that meditation might not be for everyone. My mom, for example—her type of meditation is through prayer. When she is praying, she is somewhat focused, as you would be in meditation. The good news is that if you find it difficult to meditate, there are other forms of meditation, called *moving meditations*, such as yoga, Tai Chi, and Qigong. If you are skeptical about meditation, fear not, because meditation is scientifically proven to help with overall well-being. I have read scientific studies that say if you meditate, you will live longer, healthier, and even happier. That is amazing!

Ever wonder why cats have nine lives? The answer is simple. They meditate. When I look at Abby, she seems to have two formal postures in life. First posture is the deep-sleep position. This position involves some seriously heavy sleeping. When Abby's in this position, her head is curled into her body, and she usually has her paws over her head, covering her eyes. The second posture is called the Little Buddha position. In this pose, she looks more like a lion, sitting on the prairie, with her eyes partly closed, yet still alert to sight and sound. The fur around her neck puffs up like a lion's mane. The reason I call this the Little Buddha position is because, quite frankly, she looks like she's meditating. She is in a semi-position, neither sleeping nor fully awake. Her facial expressions look focused, regardless of what's happening around her. And her breathing is slow and relaxed. Could this be the reason why, deep down in the mystical realm of the outer dimension, I was drawn to befriend a cat? Nope. I just find them cute; they require little maintenance and are easy to take care of.

Back to Happiness

It is possible to be happy, regardless of circumstances around you. You could be having a bad day, yet you could still be at peace during all the commotion. You could be living in a cave and still be happy. The sun could be shining one moment, and then, an hour later, it could be thundering, yet you still could be happy. Circumstances can change, but you still remain the same. You are still the same person before and after changing circumstances. The only thing that can change is how you react—or better yet, how you respond—to the changing circumstances.

If you've been taught to react a certain way throughout your life, then it's difficult to expect a different reaction to a changing circumstance. But if you can see your reaction for what it is—as an inherent reaction—then you can start down the path to learning how to change those reactions to responses.

There is a big difference between a reaction and a response. A reaction generally is automatic. For example, I stub my toe, and I yell in pain. There is a cause that produced an outcome. This cause and effect is like a chain reaction. As my toe hits the corner of the table, an immediate pain sensation occurs, and I react by verbally yelling in pain with a couple of swear words. A response is when the same situation occurs, except this time, I catch myself before I yell and swear, and I respond by breathing deeply into the pain. This time, no swearing! This all sounds so simple, but the truth of the matter is that it is not. Training our minds to react differently to get a more positive response takes time and practice. Anything that we want to improve on takes a lot of time and practice. Building muscles takes hours of working out in the gym every day. Learning to play the piano takes many years of lessons and practice. And so, learning to respond also takes time and practice.

If you're driving down the highway and someone cuts you off, you most likely will feel somewhat outraged. If anger develops, it can produce serious reactions. Those reactions can cause devastating effects. We've all heard of people getting into fights over these circumstances, and some situations have resulted in someone being killed. Now, imagine the same situation, driving on the highway, but this time, instead of reacting to being cut off, you respond more appropriately to prevent yourself from doing harm to yourself or others.

Our reactions can produce suffering to us and others. Learning to respond versus reacting can lead to a more peaceful solution and the road to happiness. Animals are good example of reactions versus responding. An animal reacts to a situation in the way it knows best, leading it out of danger. An animal can respond by reacting to a situation without causing further harm to itself or others. I would argue that animals react, but because they create no further action to the reaction, they're basically responding to the situation. The situation goes no further, and the animal moves on.

My cat, Abby, comes to the table, asking for food, but when she knows she's not going to receive anything, she simply reacts by turning around and walking away. There is no story, afterthought, or exchange of words. Abby simply returns to her bed and goes down for a nap. But we humans create further stories to our reactions. We get upset with changing circumstances, which then trigger more thoughts, and now we create more stories as we analyze the situation repeatedly. If we could simply learn to respond to a circumstance by letting it be, then we could let go of the story with all the attached thoughts and emotions, close our eyes, and go down for a nap.

Learning to Take a Nap

Learning to take a nap means letting go. We hear many phrases, such as, "It's no big deal," or "It's all good." But letting go is not easy, and sometimes, all is *not* good. When we see violence on TV, it's difficult to let go and say it's all good. When we see our family involved in bitter disputes over, for example, money, it's not all good. However, these phrases are helpful because they remind us to be aware, just like signposts pointing us to the correct direction.

A friend of mine once gave me a self-help book that had many tips on how to let go and not make situations worse. The book was very helpful, but I felt that I needed more guiding tools to deal with the bad things in life. When we have situations at work in which we feel we have been wronged or hurt, it's difficult to simply let go. How, then, do we learn to let go? What other signposts can we use to help with difficult situations?

One such signpost is called *awareness*. Awareness is such a powerful tool found in many themes across well-being books, spiritual teachings, and even as the basis for meditation/mindfulness practices. The logic goes something like this: when you are aware of your thoughts, then you are in the present moment, which allows you to see and choose your responses versus reacting to a situation.

When we are stressed, we are fighting between past and future. My definition of the word *stress* is fighting to have what was and wanting to have what could be. When you learn to stay in the moment, where you are not thinking of the past or the future, then letting go is possible. When you think about it, all you have is this very moment and its awareness because the past is simply the past, and the future is not even here. Why, then, do our minds not like to stay in the present moment? Have you ever tried to stay in the present moment while washing the dishes, brushing your teeth, or performing any other monotonous or dull activity? It's not easy to do, especially if your mind is not enjoying what you're doing in the present moment.

We love to think of the past, and, of course, we love to think of the future. We remember the good old times and like to dream of things to come. It's pleasurable to think of these things, especially if our current situation is difficult.

Entertaining ourselves with thoughts of the past or future has its downside. For example, thinking about that dream job, that sports car, or that big house with the perfect family of two kids and a cat creates big expectations. When things do not go our way and our expectations are not met, we get hurtfully disappointed.

With great expectations come great hurt. Please understand that I am not saying to abandon our goals; on the contrary, goals are very important. My point is that everyone needs goals, and our goals should be focused on living each step in the present moment and accomplishing each task in the present, without letting our thoughts jump to the past or future. As they say, it's the journey, not the end goal, that is important in life.

CHAPTER ONE

The Journey

When we first brought Abby into our lives, she had to contend with Peaches, our older cat. Having two cats of two different ages did not go so easy for either of them, but we felt that over time, the two would get used to each other and would eventually enjoy each other's company. When my daughter was born, Peaches had difficulty adjusting with the stress of a new person in the house. She unfortunately took to biting, and we became somewhat hesitant to keep her, for the sake of the baby's safety. Coincidentally, a friend of mine, who was a cat lover in need of company, offered to adopt Peaches. A week later, Peaches was gone. This was a very difficult and emotional decision for us. We loved Peaches, and having had her since she was a kitten made it more difficult to give her up. The only comfort we had at that time was knowing she would be taken care of.

It did not take long for Abby to adjust to the new circumstance. With Abby now free to roam the house and only contend with a newborn, life was good. But for us adults who were experiencing a newborn, life was challenging. My daughter was a colicky baby, so that meant sleepless nights for both mother and baby (and dad, of course). Sleep deprivation is stressful. Juggling a work/life balance at this time was not easy. Complicating things was that neither my wife nor I had experience or the tools for how to manage difficult situations or even how to handle our own stress. They say when the student is ready, the teacher appears. I wish the teacher had appeared back in those days to provide us with some tools to deal with those challenges. Like all people, we struggled through, and we found a way to manage.

Can you imagine if somebody approached you, early in life, and offered you a pill that would make you happy, reduce your stress, and help you deal with your worries, fears, and anxieties? There is no magic pill, but there are tools that can help you find that balance between enjoying life and surviving it. For example, *meditation* has been around for thousands of years. It can help you ground yourself in troubled times. It helps to expand your mind so that you can view thoughts and emotions nonjudgmentally. It helps you to see with more clarity and have a focused attention on things at hand. It does not take away the *bad*; it is simply a path to help you discover who you are and how to deal with life from a more balanced perspective.

One of the hardest concepts in understanding meditation is that it is not a solution to your problems; it's an opening to understanding them with sincerity. There are Buddhist monks, Zen masters, and meditation teachers who practice meditation for hours every day. It takes a lot of time to reach that level of commitment. The good news is that meditation is still possible, even when time seems limited.

In today's world, stress seems to be getting worst. Factors like job pressure, money, health, relationships, media overload, sleep deprivation, cutbacks—the list goes on—add to our stress levels. If meditation itself seems stressful due to time commitments, don't worry. In this book, both Abby and I will give you many tips and solutions to help you find your tranquility.

Finding Your Tranquility

When I think of tranquility, I think of being somewhere up North, at a cottage by the lake, listening to the birds and watching the blue sky—a tranquil setting, with the water reflecting the sunset and the green colors surrounding my place of peace. This place of tranquility exists inside all of us. The trick is to figure out how to find and tap into this inner peace. Finding peace in a troubled world is not that hard, and you don't need to look far to find it. I recall the following story of a king who was searching for the meaning of peace:

> There once lived a King who offered a prize to any artist who could paint the best picture of what peace looked like. Many artists came looking for

a chance to win this great prize. The King finally chose two pictures that he really liked. The first picture was that of a calm lake and towering in the background were snow capped mountains. Above was a blue clear sky with beautiful fluffy clouds. Everyone who saw this picture were amazed and thought certainly that this would be the picture that the King would pick. However, the King announced the winner, and it was another picture to everyone's surprise. This picture also had mountains, but the mountains were bare and rugged. The lake looked choppy because the sky above looked angry from which rain fell and lightning was in the background. Down the side of the mountain was a waterfall and behind it what a tiny bush growing in the crack of the rock. In this bush a mother bird had built her nest. Yet in the mist of the angry sky, rushing waterfall, the mother bird sat on her nest in perfect peace. Why did the King pick this picture? 'Because' explained the King. 'Peace does not mean to be in a place where there is no noise, chaos or hard work. Peace means being in the midst of all those things and still being calm in your heart and mind' (artist unknown). [1]

---

[1] Catherine Marshall, "Picture of Peace," in Stories for the Heart, ed. Alice Gray (Sisters, Oregon: Multnomah Publishers, 1996), https://frommyheart2u.wordpress.com/tag/catherine-marshall.

Whatever problems you have and whatever is going on in your life, it is possible to be at peace among it all. The mother bird in the angry sky and rushing waterfall "accepted" her circumstances and was at peace with them. Abby, in the territory of an older cat and with a newborn baby, found peace in that situation by accepting the circumstances around her. Her acceptance was demonstrated by her lying in her bed, sleeping for most of the day. Even after the occasional fight between younger Abby and older Peaches, both cats would accept what had happened, part ways, and go back to bed. Life could be so much simpler if we could accept what is and learn to relax about it.

The word *accepting* means that you allow the inner conflicts inside you to be. But this does not mean giving up on trying to change a situation. If, for example, you are being treated unfairly, then you might need to take action to ensure that you're treated justly. If you are in physical pain, your action might be to take some medication. The acceptance comes in not adding a story to the situation. It is the story you tell yourself that magnifies the issue and distorts your thinking. If in doubt as to what acceptance and peace look like, look to nature—or turn to your pet, and let him or her guide the way.

Is there a connection between happiness and being at peace? I guess it depends on your definition of happiness. If my definition of happiness is to have a scoop of chocolate-chip ice cream, what will happen to my happiness if I have four scoops of ice cream? Most likely, a lot of indigestion or upset stomach and no happiness there. That type of happiness is short-lived.

Is there a type of happiness that is long lasting and without side effects?

Recall our definition of happiness: to be at peace, calm, and in the present moment. To get to a peaceful state requires understanding of yourself. You need to understand the things that calm you down and the things that stress you out. Everybody has different tolerances to stress, and everybody has different levels of irritation. For one person, listening to music might be soothing, but for someone else, sitting by a lake and listening to the sound of the waves is peaceful. The mother bird sat in her nest in peace and let go of the sights and sounds surrounding her.

Understanding yourself takes time. The more you invest in understanding yourself, the greater insight you will have into your thinking process. Say, for example, you notice that you have a bad habit of being critical, or you always blame yourself when things go wrong. Being aware of this thinking pattern can help you to shine some light into the whys. Becoming mindful (or aware) of your thoughts can help you to see your thinking patterns. Understanding how you think can aid in creating change. Awareness and understanding are powerful tools for seeing how you think and are the keys in helping you to reach long-lasting peace or long-lasting happiness.

> There is a story of two monks who were walking through a forest. At the edge of the forest, they come to a river. Standing in front of this river was a young woman who was having difficulties

crossing it. The older monk decided to help the young woman by literally picking her up and carried her through the river to the other side. The younger monk simply watched with amazement. As they all reached the other side of the river, the young woman thanked the older monk and went her separate way. Several hours later the younger monk feeling somewhat upset said to the older monk 'why did you carry that woman across the river'? 'You know that we monks are not allowed to come in contact with women'. The older monk simply replied 'I dropped that woman hours ago. You are still carrying her.'[2]

Here is a beautiful story that illustrates understanding and awareness. The older monk understood what he had to do to help the young woman, even if it meant going against what he was taught. He was aware that as soon as he reached the other side of the river, he would be able to let go of the encounter. It was the younger monk, who lacked understanding and awareness in himself, who carried resentment in his mind and heart several hours later. One monk was able to let go and be at peace through his understanding and awareness, while the other monk was not.

When we understand that *holding on* is a reminder of something that we feel comfortable doing, we can use awareness to

---

[2] Eckhart Tolle, A New Earth: Awakening to Your Life's Purpose (New York: Penguin Random House, 2016), 139.

see how harmful this can be. The young monk who held on to his resentment for hours shows that we would rather be right than at peace. At times, we all feel comfortable holding on to something that happened to us in the past. Being offended by something that someone said or did comes easy and natural to us. It is as if we are naturally comfortable with it. Our minds like to hold on to the negative things that happen to us. Our minds like to keep track of all the bad things that occur. When we can shine awareness on this thinking, we can see how much suffering this can cause and how it can rob us of our peace.

Using awareness to see all the things that we hold on to can help us change the path to a better understanding of who we truly are. We are not our thoughts, and we are not our emotions. Our thoughts and emotions come and go, but we still remain the same. Like the young monk, if we could learn to let go, then we could learn to live in a more peaceful state. But how do we let go if our minds have the tendency to hold on? The act of letting go requires some energy. We can be aware of small things and brush them aside. We tend to hold on much tighter to the bigger things, and they are more challenging to let go. We require tools to help us through these difficult moments.

The Tool of Forgiving

My mom and dad were farmers back in the old country. Having had the experience of working with so many different animals, they had many examples to share on how animals react and respond when working with humans. My mom said that animals can feel or sense when they are loved and cared for. I personally have seen this with Abby. We have had many visitors, and, more frequently than not, Abby is drawn to animal or cat lovers. My brother, who is allergic to cats, obviously shies away from cats. Strangely enough, Abby senses this and keeps her distance from him. But if my brother were to approach her, she would not run away from him. She might be hesitant to allow him to pet her, but ultimately, she would be comfortable with him. Even though Abby is aware of my brother's lack of affection, my cat does not take it personally. It is as if Abby is able to let go of the situation.

My mom said that if you harmed an animal, the animal would always remember. And it makes sense that animals should remember to protect themselves from any further harm. Letting go does not mean forgetting something that has happened, which we might need to protect ourselves in the present moment. Burning a finger in a fire teaches us not to do that again. Remembering an event is a useful tool for protecting ourselves from further harm. When we cannot let go or forgive, that creates problems on its own. Forgiving means letting go of the act that has occurred and not associating the act to the entire situation. We do not say that fire is entirely bad but merely that the heat associated with the fire can cause harm. Similarly, when a person has done us harm, we need to forgive the act and not assume that the person is entirely bad.

We can go through our entire lives, knowing that it is better to forgive and to forget, and still not understand *how* to forgive and—even harder—*how* to forget. Some people have a natural tendency to simply forgive and forget while others struggle with the concept. To understand "forgive and forget" is easy enough, but to actually do it in practice is very difficult. I was raised as a Roman Catholic and was never taught *how* to forgive and to forget. The priest and my parents explained why I should forgive and forget, but there was no explanation of how to do it. Forgiving someone took me a long time. Letting go or trying to forget what had happened seemed impossible.

I am not saying that today I am the Buddha, but today, it takes me a shorter time to forgive and let go. I believe in my heart that each person has a natural tendency to learn how to forgive and forget. No matter who we are or what happened to us or what we did, we all have the capacity forgive and let go. This natural capacity to forgive comes in understanding two main concepts: (1) dealing with the hurt; and (2) wanting to feel good.

To heal yourself from the pain of hurtful thoughts and feelings that can keep coming back requires positive thinking. Try to understand and remember that you ultimately want to feel good. No one deserves to suffer, not you or anyone else. We all want to be happy. Every moment that you spend feeling negative takes away time when you could feel good. Ask yourself this crucial question: "Do I want to suffer less?" Yes! Now, change your thinking and answer the same question by stating, "I want to feel good." The words *I want to feel good* are an example of a tool that can help you to change your thinking.

Dr. Wayne Dyer, a spiritual author and teacher, said those five magical words: "I want to feel good!".[3] He explained that in an attempt to feel happy and to let go of anger and resentment, we need to keep repeating those words over and over again.

If you meditate, you can incorporate the phrase "I want to feel good" into a mantra, emphasizing each word as you repeat the phrase. If your emotions are very strong, you also could meditate on the emotional energy itself, trying to feel the negative emotion without any words or persons associated with the feeling. After some time, the emotion(s) should subside, and you can return to reminding yourself that you want to feel happy.

At some point, to finally remove or at least reduce your suffering (specifically, your hurtful feelings), you will need to forgive. Start by forgiving yourself for any pain that you are experiencing. Forgive yourself for any wrongdoing that you might have caused. Forgive yourself for feeling angry, spiteful, or any other negative emotion. You can repeat these words, "I forgive myself." Equally as important, you will need to forgive others. It will be difficult to forgive someone who has caused you so much pain, and you might wonder, *If I forgive, am I not just allowing myself to get hurt again?* You might not trust this person again because trust requires repeated proven behavior and action, but you can still love this person. Repeat these words: "I forgive you." Visualize in your mind that you are sending the person positive energy in the form of forgiveness. Each time you say, "I forgive you," visualize this in your mind. It can be

---

[3] Wayne W. Dyer, The Essential Wayne Dyer Collection (New York: Hay House Inc. 2013), 187.

in the form of a white light, a cool breeze, or any other comforting visualization that you can imagine. Remember, each time the hurtful feelings return, keep repeating *"I forgive you"*, and keep reminding yourself that you want to be at peace and, ultimately, happy. Once you truly feel that you have forgiven both yourself and the other person, send a blessing and wish him or her to be happy also. Releasing yourself from the hurt is the act of forgiveness, and feeling good is the transformational process of letting go.

Here is another powerful tool to help you forgive someone, especially after that person has hurt you. This tool is known as the *cultivating loving-kindness and compassion meditation practice*. In this meditation, we try to visualize and experience three states of people: a loved one, a neutral person, and an enemy.

- Start by taking a couple of deep breaths.
- Next, picture someone you truly care about. With that person in mind, try to feel love and compassion toward him or her. It might help to recollect an experience when you personally felt love and compassion toward the person.
- Now, meditate on the feelings, and with the emotions still within, you picture a neutral person whom you don't necessarily know or have any emotional connection to (e.g., a store clerk). Visualize this neutral person, and try to see and feel loving-kindness and compassion toward him or her. Stay with the feelings for a while, and see if you can wish that person to be happy.

- Next comes the difficult part, which involves picturing someone with whom you are having difficulties. At this time, many feelings will arise, such as hatred, anger, or resentment. When these emotions and feelings start to surface, it's important not to ignore them but to try to feel the actual feelings. Once the negative energy is at a calming state or has subsided, try once again to visualize the person. If you need to do so, go back to visualize the neutral person or go back farther to the loved one, and try to generate loving-kindness and compassionate feelings again.
  - We are trying to bring positive emotions or energy and use them to help cultivate the same energy toward the difficult person. When we can see that the difficult person is no longer an enemy but a person who, like us, experiences suffering, we can learn to feel compassion for that person. Try to remember that unmindful words and actions come about when someone is suffering or simply because of his or her ego. In other words, look past the unmindful action to see the person as someone like you. We all want to feel good and avoid suffering. This is something that every human being has in common, and understanding this helps us to connect with people and relate to their feelings. When we can relate to people and their feelings, then forgiveness becomes easier.

This type of meditation helps you to transform your hurt into wanting to feel good so that you can forgive and let go. Timothy Barlow, a good friend of mine, wrote,

> Forgiveness is not about releasing them, it's about releasing yourself from the pain of anger and resentment and transforming it into empathy and understanding.[4]

Letting Go of the Story. The Ego

The house in which we lived when we first brought Abby into our lives had a small fenced-in backyard. We would usually let Abby roam free in the backyard but supervised. One day, I let Abby outside and then decided to go back into the house to do a couple of things. Shortly afterward, I came back out to check on Abby, and I found another cat in the backyard. I watched as both cats hissed at each other. Then Abby began to growl at the intruder and moved forward, as if to defend her territory. When I realized that a fight might ensue, I decided to intervene. I chased away the other cat and came back to Abby to give her some comfort and reassurance that all was OK. Five minutes later, Abby went back into the house as if nothing had happened. As for me, I looked again to make sure that the other cat had left and wasn't returning. I called my wife and told her the story. That evening,

---

[4] Timothy Barlow, "It's All Good: Forgiveness comes easier if you forgive yourself first," Vaughan Citizen, April 23, 2014, 1.

I told the cat-intruder story to a friend. This was not, however, what happened to Abby. Abby simply walked away as if nothing had happened. Abby had the ability to *forgive* the intruder and let go of the event. There was no sense of holding on to the story that had unfolded in the backyard. How was Abby able to let go of the story and return to the present moment? As humans, how can we do the same?

Letting go of a story requires many factors. We first need to be aware of our thinking; specifically, *ruminative thinking*. The first step in the process of letting go is to become mindful of seeing our thoughts repeating and to become aware of when our emotions get activated. Next, we need to deal with our emotions that get activated, especially if they become strong emotions, such as anger, resentment, hatred, jealousy, worry, or fear. Think of these feelings and emotions as built-up charged energy. If we do nothing, the energy simply sits within us, manifesting itself into other problems. But if we can deal with these emotions in a positive way, then we can learn to transform this charged energy into a more peaceful and calming state. We can transform these strong emotions by using tools such as mindfulness and meditation.

We need to feel through the emotions, rather than working against the emotions. Think of it as shown in the following example: It is harder to swim against the tide than to swim with the tide. When you learn how to swim with the tide, you go through the wave and easily emerge on the other side, instead of resisting the waves. It is important to deal with our emotions; otherwise, our emotions will create more thoughts, and the story will continue to repeat itself. By having a handle on our emotions and thoughts, we can reduce them to a more workable and peaceful state. Awareness plays a big part in this process by catching our minds that want to replay the story. When we become more aware, we can learn how to let go of the story versus replaying the story.

Going back to the cat-intruder story, my mind needed to replay and retell the story. At the time, it felt pleasant to tell someone what had happened. I say *pleasant* because it felt like a form of release, at first, to get it off my chest. But then, several hours later, while I was watching TV, the story came back into my mind, out of nowhere, bringing with it all the thoughts and emotions again. Obviously, I still felt somewhat bothered from the experience, but why? I still felt the need or the drive to tell the story again.

Think about a time when someone said something to you that made you feel hurt or offended. What thoughts were in your mind afterward? If you told someone what happened to you, try to recollect the words you used when you repeated your story. The most common words are generally *I* and *me* in each sentence. For example, you might hear yourself saying:

"I can't believe what he said to me."

"I was so upset by what she did."

"They have no consideration for me."

"He was so rude to me."

"Next time, I'm not going to take her remarks. I'm going to say something."

"They didn't even call to congratulate me."

"I worked so hard, and he didn't even say thank you."

"I have such bad luck."

"I can't believe how lucky they are."

The words *I* and *me* are descriptive words associated to our egos. The ego keeps the story alive. Let me explain:

We all have an image of who we are. We define ourselves (ego identification) through the stage in life we are in or the type of work or profession we do. We can be, for example, students, parents, workers, professionals, or athletes. When the image of ourselves becomes the definition of who we are, then we create ego (or self-image, pride). This ego begins to grow as we add descriptive behaviors of ourselves. For example, I am a good and strict parent. We can easily become defensive to someone's remarks and advice and perceive them as judgments or accusations because we are defending a mental image of who we are.

Say, for example, you are speaking to someone, and he or she comments on your weight. Depending on the person and the intent of the comment, you might feel hurt, resentful, or confused. The need to defend yourself might arise from many reasons (e.g., it's difficult to lose or gain weight due to your body type, health, or stress level). In this example, as the comment is made, our egos will be engaged. The comment will produce a thought that will lead to an emotion, which will feed into the ego. As the ego is engaged, more thoughts and more hurtful feelings will arise, and so the story begins, and we get a never-ending story.

In the scenario of the backyard cat intruder, my ego was engaged, and my story was something like this: I can't believe that people don't know how to keep an eye on their pets. My cat might have been hurt by the intruder. I care about my Abby. How dare it be that my cat can't be free to wander in her own backyard. I'd better let my neighbors know of this cat intrusion and warn them not to leave their pets alone in the backyard. Wait until I tell my friends about this.

My ego, or my need to be right and defend my mental position, kept this story alive. My fear and worry over my cat's safety also emotionally fueled my thoughts. In essence, I experienced suffering. I was not at peace, and my mind was not calm. In reality, there were two cats that communicated to each other in their language. That is the only story here.

If we can remove the need to defend our mental position or our image of who we are, then we can learn not to react to our egos. This, in turn, will allow our minds to be in a calm state; thus, we will be able to control our reactions and respond more appropriately. Here are some steps on how to let go of your ego:

- **Step 1: Recognize**. Recognize that your mind automatically takes over as it reacts to the situation or hurtful comment. At this crucial time, try to be mindful of this automatic mind reaction.
- **Step 2: Understand.** Understand that by reacting, you will only cause the situation to get worse. Treat the feelings, emotions, and thoughts that arise from the defensive ego by first recognizing that your mind is simply trying to defend a mental position.

- **Step 3: Breathe.** In this moment, take a couple of deep breaths to help yourself not to react. Close your eyes, if the situation permits. You may find counting out ten breaths helpful. Imagine the breath entering your nose into your belly, and as you breathe out, imagine the breath going out of your belly and out of your nose.
- **Step 4: Choice.** You have the choice to respond instead of react. If someone has said something hurtful, you can choose to acknowledge the person's comment, excuse yourself, and walk away. If you decide to stay, try putting an end to the comment and move on to the next topic. If you feel that you need to respond, rather than a defensive or offensive comment, try a loving-compassionate comment, such as, "I think you are a better person than that."
- **Step 5: Neutralize.** In the end, you will need to deal with the feelings and emotions that arise. Once the conversation or situation is over, spend some time in meditation (e.g., focusing on your breath to feel the emotions to help lessen the charged energy). You ultimately want to neutralize the emotions and try to feel good again.
- **Step 6: Patience and Kindness.** Dealing with the ego and changing your thought patterns is very difficult, as the ego is embedded in your nature. Give yourself generous amounts of patience, kindness, and compassion when handling the ego.

When we learn to become aware of our egos, we can learn to focus on the story but also to deal with our thoughts and emotions with more clarity. There are times, however, when retelling a story might be necessary to gain some insight or clarity or to get an opinion. In such situations, it seems OK to retell the story to a friend or an expert.

Next time you need to retell a story, ask yourself the following questions: (1) Am I still reacting to what happened? (2) Am I still emotionally upset by the events that occurred? (3) Do I need to defend a mental position?

If your thoughts and emotions are still engaged, and you need to defend a mental position, then go back and repeat the six helpful steps mentioned above on how to let go of your ego. The reason to ask yourself these three questions is to help you to gain some awareness of your thoughts and emotions so that you can respond appropriately. And whatever answers you get, be sure to respond with compassion and kindness toward yourself versus self-criticism or unrealistic expectations from yourself.

Remember that we want to bring our minds back to a state of peace, which we defined as happiness.

CHAPTER TWO

Dealing with Unpleasantry to Get Back to Clarity and Peace

When we get hurt, our thoughts and emotions feed into the ego, and we get more thoughts and more hurtful feelings. How do we stop or slow down this circle of unpleasantry? The answer is with less storytelling and emotional identification and greater awareness to our sensations. There are three levels to storytelling. The first level is the *story*. The second level is *emotions*. And the third level is *interoceptive awareness*.

The first level—the bottom level—is the story. As we progress upward, we identify with our emotions. And finally, at the top we have interoceptive awareness, where we connect the emotions to the sensations in our bodies (for example, "I felt my heart pounding in my chest"). Progressing upward requires better self-regulation and a greater sense of awareness in the moment.

The following is an example how this works. At level 1, the story might sound something like this: "I can't believe that people don't know how to keep an eye on their pets. If I hadn't intervened, my cat might have been hurt by the intruder." At level 2, emotions, I might say, "I was upset and anxious when I realized that the intruder cat was going to hurt my Abby." Level 3 is interoceptive awareness: "I felt a sudden uneasiness in my stomach."

As we move from level 1 to level 3, we start to remove storytelling and shift our focus to our emotions. Once we start identifying how we feel, then the next step is to focus our attention on *where* we feel these emotions or sensations within the body. At level 1, we are very good at retelling our stories. Level 1 might be where our egos best survive. As we move to level 2 and focus on our emotions, we ask ourselves, "How do I feel?" in relation to the story. It is here where we answer with "I feel ... (angry, insulted, worried, scared, nervous, anxious, offended)." By spending some time in level 2, we begin to understand which emotions we are feeling. In focusing our attention on our emotions, we remove ourselves from storytelling. The greater the time that we spend in seeking to understand our feelings, the farther we distance ourselves from storytelling.

Once we have identified how we feel, we begin to understand what type of emotions we are experiencing. When we identify the emotions, we can now move to level 3, where we take the emotional experience, or feeling, and look where *in* the body these emotions are expressed. For example, if I'm feeling nervous, I might feel this as butterflies in my stomach. If I'm feeling angry, I might feel my face flush. Level 3 is where we focus our awareness and our attention to the actual sensations (e.g., butterfly feeling, hot sensation). With greater attention and focus on bodily sensations, we remove storytelling. There can be no story when we focus our attention on investigating where in the body we feel the sensations.

We will explore interoceptive awareness in greater depth in the upcoming chapter.

Learning Mindfulness and Meditation

Moving from storytelling (level 1) to emotional identification (level 2) and finally to interoceptive awareness (level 3) requires mindfulness and meditation. Mindfulness and meditation contain three elements to help us reduce storytelling and get back to clarity by providing (1) awareness, (2) focused concentration, and (3) emotional identification. Another word for *awareness* is *mindfulness*. Another word for *focused concentration* is *meditation*. And lastly, through mindfulness and meditation, we learn to recognize and deal with, in a healthy manner, our *emotions*. In other words, mindfulness and meditation are the tools needed to get clarity and peace to bring back happiness.

Mindfulness

Mindfulness helps us to become aware of our thoughts, feelings, and actions in the present moment. Experts say that our minds produce fifty thousand thoughts a day, or 2,100 thoughts per hour. With so many thoughts per day, which thoughts do we act upon and which do we ignore? With the practice of mindfulness, we can learn how to "see" our thoughts and become more aware of them. We can learn to choose which thoughts to ignore and which to act upon. When we are able to see our thoughts, we can learn to become more aware of living our lives to the fullest possibilities by being and living in the present moment.

For example, when we become irritated or stressed, mindfulness can help us see our thoughts and emotions. Instead of reacting in an automatic or negative way, mindfulness can help by allowing us to see more options and to respond more appropriately to irritation and stress. Mindfulness also teaches us to notice our thoughts and emotions in a nonjudgmental way, so we are at peace with whatever is and whatever is to become. When the mind is without self-awareness, unmindful thoughts can lead to hurtful words and actions that create suffering to both ourselves and others.

Learning how to become mindful entails patience and practice as you become more aware of your thoughts, feelings, and actions. Try this activity: close your eyes and take a slow, deep breath. Try to visualize your breath as it enters your nose and throat. See the breath enter your lungs, and watch the breath as it exits your throat and out from your nose. It is important to go as slowly as you can. A slow outer breath also can help you to relax more. You also might picture the air entering your nose and then feel the sensation of the air. The sensation of the air can be felt in or at the beginning of the nostril or whichever part of the nose is easiest and most comfortable for you to feel. Now try taking five more breaths, and each time, visualize or feel the movement of the air with your attention on the breath.

Take a minute to explore how you felt during this breathing exercise. For example, was it difficult to focus your attention on the breath, or was it easy? Try it again!

Ask yourself these questions:

1. What thoughts came into my mind while I was breathing?
2. Did any images pop into my mind?
3. Did I experience any emotions or feelings?
4. Did I have any sensations (for example, an itch or some discomfort)?
5. Did I hear any sounds or notice any smells?

- For the next part of this activity, take another five to six breaths with your eyes closed, but this time try *not* to focus your attention on the breath. Try it now! Again, ask yourself the same five questions above.
- Here is another activity to try: With your eyes open this time, stare at a blank wall for a minute. Try it! How did you feel? Was the experience comfortable or uncomfortable? Were you able to sit still, or did you feel the need to move or scratch an itch? Do you remember any thoughts you had in that minute?

Dealing with Unpleasantry to Get Back to Clarity and Peace

- Try the above activity again, but this time, as you stare at the blank wall, focus on your breath. Try this for about a minute. Did fewer or more thoughts come into your mind while you focused on your breath?

Did any of the above activities seem easier when you were concentrating on your breath? If your answer was yes, it was most likely because your mind was preoccupied with the breath. If you found that staring at the wall was easier than putting your attention on the breath, this was probably because your mind's attention was on the wall itself (e.g., focusing on the color, texture, etc.). When our minds are focused on something, we generally have fewer scattered thoughts. In mindfulness, when we use the mind's attention to view our thoughts, we can learn to allow thoughts to come and go without chasing them or feeding into them. A thought that comes and goes is *one thought* without any additional scattered thoughts.

How Does Meditation Help? What Is the Connection to Mindfulness?

Imagine that your mind is a vast ocean, with seemingly endless water and depth. On some days, storms rage, and on other days, calmness exists. Mindfulness allows us to view whatever is on the surface, while meditation brings us below the surface to a deep, quiet, and calm realm. Meditation allows us to go deep into the mind to train the brain and rewire its synaptic hardware, to allow us to focus and concentrate better.

With meditation, you can change your brain and change your thoughts to a calmer and more peaceful mind. Meditation allows you to learn more of what is already present in you, of which you are not aware. By spending time in yourself, you invest time in becoming a better you.

Meditation Practice

There are many ways to practice meditation. One of the simplest forms is following your breath. You focus on the in-and-out motion of the breath to help steady the thoughts and ultimately calm the mind. When you are ready to begin meditation, remind yourself that you are allowing your mind to focus on the breath and that there is no outcome, in the sense of competing or achieving some type of perfection state. As you practice, it is normal that something will arise to disturb your meditation (e.g., sounds, an itch, a muscle cramp, a repeating thought, a visual thought pattern, an emotion), and when this happens, you need to have patience and compassion for yourself. Learning anything new requires a lot of patience. Having compassion for yourself allows you to drop any expectations of yourself and to see the experience as only an experience versus an extension of your character.

For example, if thoughts or emotions keep arising during your mediation practice, understand that you are not the cause of it but rather your mind. Understanding the concept that you are not in control of what your mind and body create (e.g., thoughts, an itch, etc.) will allow you to give permission to yourself to be patient and compassionate toward yourself and toward your practice. If your mind generates thoughts and feelings that you are doing something wrong or that meditation is too difficult, remind yourself and reinforce that, with practice and patience, that will pass. Furthermore, that can teach you a lot about yourself by showing you what you need to work on. With practice, your mind will become more peaceful, and with patience, you will find that fewer things trouble you.

When you practice meditation, find a quiet area that will help you to focus, free from outside distractions. Keep your practice short. Try to practice many times throughout the day. If you can set up a routine, the better it will be for you, as this will then become a habit. I have heard that it takes up to two months for your brain to create a habit. Likewise, it will take two months of meditation practice for it to become a long and, hopefully, a lifelong habit.

Early morning, midafternoon, and just before bed tend to be my choices of habit. Early in the morning is a great time to practice because as you wake up, there are fewer processing activities going on in your mind. In the middle of the day, try to find an opportunity to practice to help your mind stay focused and to keep your mind at peace. In the evening before bed might be a good time to practice to help your mind calm down before sleeping.

Many positions or choices are available to help you to feel

comfortable when doing your meditation. For example, the Buddha is usually pictured sitting on the ground in a cross-legged fashion (called the lotus position). Pick a posture or position in which you feel comfortable. If you find it painful or uncomfortable to sit and meditate on the floor, try sitting in a chair. You could sit on the couch with a pillow below each knee to raise the knees, thereby putting less strain on the upper leg muscles. If you prefer lying down to meditate, keep your back as comfortable as possible. For example, putting a pillow behind your knees will help your back feel more comfortable, especially if you have back pain. If you find yourself nodding off or falling asleep, this can be your body and mind telling you that you need more sleep. Meditation will reveal what is already present in you now that you are not aware of.

What type of meditation fits you? There are many different types of meditation practices: breathing (following the breath, belly/deep breathing), body scan (scanning the body), listening, walking, etc. Each type of meditation practice helps the mind to focus, concentrate, and increase patience and tolerance, which all lead to a more peaceful and calmer mind.

Begin with breathing meditation when learning to meditate. It is important to start with breathing because breathing is what we do all the time. Even though we naturally breathe, we need to learn how to breath when we practice meditation. For example, there is belly breathing or deep breathing, which most of us do not do, but babies do it naturally. In belly breathing, you take slow, deep breathes through your nose and expand your belly. Put your hands just below your rib cage to help you feel your belly (or your diaphragm, which is why it is also called diaphragmatic breathing) move as you breathe. With each slow, deep breath, try to push your hands forward to help feel your belly rise. As you breathe out, try to release the air as slowly as you can (the slower the better).

This type of breathing is very beneficial when you need help to reach deep states of relaxation and regain your calmer true self. Even learning to take five to ten deep mindful breaths throughout the day is practicing breathing meditation. Sitting in your car, waiting for a green light, is an opportunity for deep breathing. Waiting at the cashier provides patient breathing. And the restroom offers a quick opportunity to practice meditation.

If you look for opportunities to practice, you will find them everywhere. And once breathing meditation becomes a habit and you become more comfortable with it, you can try exploring other types of meditation to help deepen your meditation experience.

Body Scan Meditation

Body scan meditation is great for helping to recognize any tension you might have in your body. In body scan meditation, you begin by taking several deep breaths, and shift your focus on examining your body. Learning to recognize the tension helps you to stop what you are doing, which prevents any further harm, and then apply relaxation techniques to help you relax the tension.

- To begin, pick a posture or position in which you feel comfortable. You can sit on a chair, or you can do this practice on the floor. If you prefer lying down, keep your back as comfortable as possible. For example, putting a pillow behind your knees will help your back feel more comfortable, especially if you have back pain. In this practice, you will bring awareness to your body to help recognize any tension that you might be experiencing.
- Begin by taking several deep breaths (slow in and slow out). Notice the breath, and notice how you feel.
- Now shift your attention to belly breathing. Remember to take slow, deep breaths through your nose, and expand your belly. It's always helpful to put your hands just below your rib cage to help you feel your belly move as you breathe. With each slow, deep breath, try to feel your hands push forward to help you feel your belly rise. As you breathe out, try to release the air as slowly as you can (the slower the better).
- Now shift your attention to begin scanning your body.

    o Start with the top of your head. Visualize the top of your head, and see if you can get a sense to feel your scalp and scan your hair (or the weight of your hair).
    o Next, focus on your face (your eyes, your eyebrows, the muscles surrounding your eyes, the mouth, the jaw), and see if there is any tension. If your mind starts to wander (and our minds

normally do) gently bring back your attention to scanning. You are training your mind to be attentive, and to do this, you need to be gentle with yourself. Kindness brings about change, while harshness only causes the mind to rebel.

- Again, take a few deep breaths. Once you are done, continue scanning below your head (your neck, shoulders, left arm, right arm).
- Now, scan your back (upper, middle, and lower back). Again, if your mind starts to wander, bring it gently and lovingly back to the breath. If, at any point, an emotion arises, simply allow the emotion to be present and just notice it as best as you can. No need to get into a fight with yourself over it. There is no need to analyze it or figure out why it is there. If it helps, remind yourself that you are not your thoughts, emotions, or feelings but a being who notices these things.
- Continue scanning the lower part of your body (your thighs, the right leg, and finally the left leg).
- Next, go back to the breath, and slowly breathe in and slowly breathe out, focusing your attention on the breath. Do this for one minute.
- When you are finished, open your eyes and ask yourself, "How do I feel now?"
- Great work!

- **Note**: If, at any point, you sense tension in a specific part of your body, try to focus your concentration on that area for a minute. Try not to be alarmed or worried if the tension worsens in that minute of concentration. This means that you have found yourself at a heightened state of awareness, noticing the details of the tension. We generally don't realize this tension throughout the day because our minds are distracted with other things. The tension itself might start to change during this minute. And this is OK. Generally, the tension should start slowly and diminish somewhat. If it helps, try to visualize white healing light entering your body through your nose and making its way into the area of tension. Visualize this white light healing the area of tension. Continue to do this for another minute. If you find that the tension becomes overwhelming, stop your concentration and go back to focusing on your breathing.

Listening Meditation

If you feel that certain sounds or sounds in general are a source of noise to you, which create some type of discomfort, you can practice listening meditation. It is important to understand that all sounds are just sounds. Our minds categorize them as either good or bad, annoying or pleasant. Listening to the sound of waves while trying to fall asleep can be a comfort for someone but a disruption for someone else. Have you ever noticed that some people are able to fall asleep, regardless of the sounds around them? For example, a windy night is a pleasing sound for someone but a source of noise for someone else. By practicing listening meditation, you can learn to calm your mind to accept sounds in a nonjudgmental way. This form of meditation takes time, but with daily practice, you will allow your thinking patterns in your brain to change. This does not mean that all sounds will no longer bother you, but you will learn to adjust and allow greater patience with all sources of sounds.

Try this listening meditation practice:

- Begin by taking five slow, deep breaths.
- Now try to pick out one constant sound, and listen to that sound without any judgment. For example, if you are outside, you can listen to the wind, the background sound of distant traffic, an air conditioner running, birds chirping, etc. It's easier to work with a sound that constantly produces noise; that way, you can focus on the continuous sound.
    - As you are listening, thoughts, judgments, emotions, feelings, or anything else may arise. Simply go back to listening each time your mind wanders.

- - Try this for two to three minutes.
- Next, go back to the breath, and slowly breathe in and slowly breathe out, focusing your attention on the breath.
  - Do this for one minute.
- Great work!

At first, you might want to try this activity for a few minutes. With more practice, you can increase the amount of time, and, eventually, your mind will settle easier to accept sounds with a less bothersome feeling.

Walking Meditation

If you are outside and need to take a mind break, try walking meditation. Walking meditation is very helpful to calm your mind by focusing on your steps. You can try walking meditation indoors if you are walking long distances. In walking meditation, you concentrate on the motion of your foot, focusing on the sensation as the foot begins touching the ground, feeling the heel-to-toe motion. You can focus on one foot or alternate on both. Pick a pace that's most comfortable for you to meditate on the sensation or motion, to help calm the mind. If you have the opportunity, pick a place to walk that has few distractions (e.g., a quiet sidewalk or trail). Before you begin, take a couple of deep breaths to help in the transition into walking meditation and calming the mind.

Compassion and Kindness for Yourself

Learning mindfulness and meditation needs to be coupled with compassion and kindness toward yourself. When you encounter obstacles in practicing mindfulness and meditation, such as those in dealing with strong thoughts and emotions, it is important to have compassion and kindness toward yourself. Even when dealing with life's difficulties, the road to peace is through compassion and kindness. This means being friendly, gentle, and tender toward yourself with the desire to be free from suffering and the causes of suffering. Have you ever seen an animal being cruel and unkind to itself? I have never seen Abby being harsh or unkind to herself. Animals do not go through the internal dialogue of beating themselves up when something goes wrong or when encountering life's obstacles. When Abby cleans herself, she also shows gentleness, kindness, and compassion toward herself by gently licking her fur. This type of action is her way of saying, *It's OK. All is good.*

Ask yourself if any struggle or problem that you've encountered has ever been solved by being harsh with yourself. If a friend or a family member had the same struggle or problem, would you be harsh with them? The road to peace is in being kind to yourself, as you would be kind to a dear friend or family member. Sometimes we think that if we are harsh toward ourselves, this will help motivate us to change our behavior or the outcome. Setting unrealistic expectations only creates disappointment and discouragement when we do not meet these standards. Furthermore, using words such as *I should*, *I shouldn't*, *I must*, or *I mustn't* can lead to feelings of failure when things don't go our way.

Recognize that your mind and body are imperfect and that every human being is broken in some way. Because of this, you cannot blame or be harsh with yourself. You were not equipped to handle every obstacle, problem, or situation with a perfect outcome or result. When you make a mistake on a test, the answer is marked wrong. Just because the answer was wrong, however, doesn't mean that there is something wrong with you. A wrong answer could simply mean that you did not have the knowledge to answer the question correctly. Later, when realizing the mistake, it's easy to say, I *should've* picked the correct answer. Once again, when you use words such as *I should have* or *I could have*, they lead to unrealistic expectations. If your lotto numbers did not win, what is the point in saying, "I should've picked a different set of numbers"?

The point is that our minds and bodies are imperfect, and this allows us not to handle situations and problems perfectly or with a desired outcome. Your not knowing the correct lotto numbers this week does not mean that there is something wrong with you; it means that there is nothing wrong with you. The road to happiness is in showing compassion and kindness toward yourself.

A powerful method that I use in both my meditation and mindfulness is from a teaching by Tara Brach, an American psychologist, author, and meditation teacher. She explains that we should whisper caring messages to ourselves, such as "It's

OK," "It's not your fault," "I'm sorry," and "I love you." She mentions that we should gently place our hands on our hearts or cheeks to help with the healing process. This might seem odd to us, only because we are not used to showing ourselves compassion and kindness. We need self-compassion and kindness to help us build the foundation for successfully addressing our obstacles in meditation—and in life, in general.

Using Compassion and Kindness to Deal with Unpleasantry

Since our minds and bodies are imperfect, and every human being is broken in some way, there is no need to blame or to be harsh with ourselves when dealing with unpleasantry. By practicing meditation, we learn how to effectively work with unpleasantry, rather than expending energy trying to fight against it. By practicing mindfulness, we learn how to experience the present moment in a nonjudgmental way. This means having the mindset of being compassionate and kind to ourselves, rather than judging ourselves harshly. By bringing ourselves to a more balanced mind, we can accept what is happening and, thus, rest in a calmer state.

So how do you use compassion and kindness to deal with unpleasantry? Say, for example, you are upset with yourself for something you did. It could be something such as losing your temper and raising your voice to your spouse or children. It could be something that you didn't do or you believed you failed to do. As an example, someone spoke to you harshly, and later, you felt that you should have defended yourself by speaking up. Or you were doing a task, and things didn't go your way, which led to feelings of disappointment and frustration.

It is during these times that we need to use mindfulness to catch ourselves when we are thinking and feeling out of character. And when we use tools such as meditation or something as simple as taking five deep breaths to help calm our minds, we can then introduce kindness and compassion as one of these tools to bring ourselves back to a more balanced mind.

Whenever you feel frustrated, disappointed, hurt, afraid, or worried, recognize in yourself that it's not easy to be human. It's not easy to deal with life's constant changes. Recognize that you are not equipped, both in mind and body, to deal successfully with all of life's changes, obstacles, and challenges.

The good news is that we are equipped with an abundance of kindness and compassion, available to us at anytime. This great source is what gets us through the frustrations, hurts, and disappointments. The act of compassion is the act of recognizing that we are in a state of suffering, and we wish ourselves to be happy. The act of kindness is the act of acknowledging that we humans are not perfect. We acknowledge this by saying kind words to ourselves (e.g., "It's OK. I am human and not perfect. I love myself"). Basically, we create a state of mind (called compassion), followed by a state of action (called kindness). It is through these two states that we deal with unpleasantry to get us back to a more balanced mind.

Tapping into and Creating an Abundance of Compassion and Kindness

Tapping into and creating an abundance of compassion and kindness requires practice. Anything in life in which you want to get better requires some form of practice. When it comes to compassion and kindness, the more you practice, the greater your abundance becomes. Here is an activity to try once a day; it takes only three to five minutes:

- **Step 1:** Begin by picking a posture or position that makes you feel comfortable. (You can sit on a chair or lie on the floor.)
- **Step 2:** Take a couple of deep breaths (slow in, slow out). Notice the breath, breathing here in this moment.
- **Step 3:** Send kindness and compassion to yourself. Repeat these words on the out breath: "May I feel happy." Repeat this a total of five times.
- **Step 4:** Repeat these words on the out breath: "May I avoid suffering and the causes of suffering." Repeat this a total of five times.
- **Step 5:** Picture someone you truly care about. With that person in mind, try to feel love, compassion, and kindness toward him or her. It might help to recollect an experience when you personally felt compassion toward the person. Try to generate the emotion and feel it. With the feeling in your mind, say the words: "May

you feel happy and avoid suffering." Repeat this a total of five times.

- **Step 6:** Take a couple of slow, deep breaths (slow in, slow out). How do you feel?

CHAPTER THREE

Even Abby Can Get Frustrated

Picture a room in which the only entrance to it is a bullet-proof glass door that is locked. Picture yourself outside the room, looking through the glass door at your car keys and house keys on a table behind this door. To make matters worse, you are late for your wedding. Forget about breaking the glass to get your keys because it's bullet-proof. Got the picture?

This is how my cat, Abby, feels each time our study room door is closed. Our study room has a glass door (minus the bullet-proof part). Any time anyone is in this room with the door closed, Abby goes out of her mind. It is as if demons have possessed her and are torturing her. She first stands in front of the door, meowing. The meowing sounds like this in human language: "Open the door! *Please* open the door!" If the door remains closed, she then becomes possessed and wails on the floor, flipping from side to side, meowing the entire time. Once the door opens, it is business as usual, and the demons go away, and my cat is back to normal. She will enter the room, look, and, a minute later, leave as if nothing ever happened.

When Abby received the memo that day that the study room door would be closed, she did not deal with the situation with equanimity. Instead, she became frustrated with the situation. She saw that the door was closed and had issues accepting this fact. She could have been analyzing and trying to figure out why the door was closed when it usually is open. And unfortunately, poor Abby was probably grasping the past, remembering when the door was kept open. From Abby's reaction, we could see that having the door closed was a bad thing. Like Abby, when we don't get our way, we too can become agitated, frustrated, irritated, and even angry. Is there a way through when life's doors are closed to us?

Let's start with the door itself. Imagine a physical door that represents life's imperfections. These imperfections can be our problems or challenges. When the door is closed, our minds try to figure out why. The mind needs to solve problems to get to an answer or conclusion—this is what minds do best. Our minds are not good with confusion or when we cannot figure out the *whys*. Our minds like to judge things as either good or bad. When we are trying to analyze things as either good or bad, we create suffering for ourselves. If we can learn to see things as they *are* or neutral, then we can remove ourselves from analyzing, or we can grasp the way things should be.

The following story illustrates that we do not truly know the consequences of good things versus bad things in life:

> A farmer had a horse that ran away one day. The neighbors said to the farmer, "Oh, how unlucky you are." The farmer simply replied, "Maybe." The next week, the farmer's horse came back and with it brought wild horses that followed. The neighbors commented to the farmer saying, "Oh, how lucky you are that you not only have one but now several horses." The farmer simply replied, "Maybe." That same week the farmer's son was trying to break one of the horses when it threw him to the ground, and the son broke his leg from the fall. The neighbors said, "Oh, what bad luck you have." But the farmer simply replied, "Maybe." A few weeks later soldiers came to the village to recruit all the boys. But when the soldiers came to the farmer's house, they saw that the son had a broken leg and decided not to take him. The neighbors once again said, "How fortunate you are that your son got spared." To which the farmer simply replied, "Maybe." [5]

When doors are closed, it might seem like a misfortune, but like the wise farmer in the story, who knew that we can never

---

[5] Alan Watts, "The Story of the Chinese Farmer," https://www.craftdeology.com/the-story-of-the-chinese-farmer-by-alan-watts, accessed 11/8/21.

know the entire story, good can become bad, and bad can become good. Simply accepting things without judgment brings us to a state of equanimity. A calm response or a tranquil pose allows us to be at peace, regardless of the situation at hand. You might think, *Yes, I understand this concept, but it's not an easy one to do.* And you would be correct. Life is not perfect, and our minds are not perfect. So what can you do when you find yourself in front of a closed door?

Try this: Instead of analyzing to either solve the problem or determine if things are good or bad, give compassion and kindness to yourself when dealing with the conflict, confusion, and suffering. Acknowledge and give self-care to yourself. Be mindful, which will help to stop you from analyzing or problem-solving. If this seems difficult, then simply be gentle and accept yourself. Don't respond to your thoughts; instead, watch them nonjudgmentally. Picture breathing in calming white light and breathing out your negative thoughts in the form of gray or black smoke.

Looking back at the story, even when the farmer seemed to have good fortune, he still responded with "Maybe." If someone came up to me and said that I had good luck because I'd won a luxurious sports car or a two-week all-inclusive vacation, could I respond with, "Maybe"? I would automatically think that luck was on my side and that this was good fortune (who wouldn't?). The problem is that we can get ourselves into the trap of what is called *grasping*. Grasping is when we try to hold on to the past or future or to an experience. When we do this, we can encounter suffering in the way of frustration. Here are some examples to illustrate grasping:

"I should be like this."

"I should think like this."

"My health should be like this."

"My relationship is perfect."

"I feel useless now."

"Things were better in the past."

"Once I find my dream job, everything will be perfect."

"I don't understand why my son has changed."

Trying to hold on to an experience or a past or future event prevents us from living in the moment. Have you ever heard of the monkey coconut trap? To trap a monkey, hunters would cut a hole in a coconut and place a piece of fruit inside. One end of the coconut would be tied to a tree. The hole would be big enough for the monkey to put its hand inside but not big enough to get its fist out. As the monkey put its hand inside, it would make a fist to hold on to the fruit but then couldn't pull out its fist. Because the monkey did not want to let go of the fruit, it got trapped and caught by the hunters.

Just like the monkey, we can trap ourselves and get caught by suffering by not letting go of the things that we hold on to. In Abby's case, her "coconut" was, *The door should always be open.* Try to think about what things you might be holding on to. Are you holding on to a grudge? Are you holding on to a fear or worry? If you can just let go of your coconut, you can be free and at peace.

The Coffee Mug

I once had a perfect coffee mug. It held the exact amount of coffee that I enjoyed to drink. It was made of a ceramic material that was smooth, and it kept the coffee warm. The mug was a gift, so I cherished it because it had meaning to me. I had this coffee mug for several years and enjoyed using it almost every day. One day, as I was sitting at my desk, my hand accidentally caught the tip of the mug and caused it to fall over, breaking it into two pieces. I was furious at myself and, of course, upset at the situation. But then I remembered two important phrases: (1) have no expectations, and (2) all things pass.

Remembering these two phrases allowed me to let go of my frustration in breaking the mug and in blaming myself. When I first got this mug, I thought that it would stay with me forever. The problem is that I had an expectation that was unrealistic. Other than breaking the mug, it could have been lost or stolen. This unrealistic expectation is what led me to become frustrated. In essence, I was holding on to this expectation.

And the second phrase—all things pass—means that everything must change because nothing can ever stay the same. The term to describe such a phrase is *impermanence*. In life, there is the ongoing process of living and dying. All living forms and all materials change over time. Nothing lasts forever; everything changes and eventually decays. Impermanence also applies to my coffee mug. My coffee mug could not last forever because, eventually, it would change—break, be lost, be stolen, or, in a thousand years, decay over time.

Impermanence also applies to Abby's study room door. The door is either open or closed; it is never the same. Impermanence also applies to the farmer and his changing circumstances. One day he has one horse, and the very next week, he has several. Impermanence also applies to the farmer's son. One day he is healthy, and the next day he is lying in bed with a broken leg. Nothing lasts forever.

This does not mean you can't enjoy what you have or enjoy an experience; if anything, it means that you need to appreciate every moment of life, knowing that nothing lasts forever. Even our thoughts and emotions change. One moment, we are happy, and the next, we are sad.

> There's a story of a King who offered a reward to anyone that could give him great wisdom to help him deal with life's challenges. Many people came and offered advice, but none that helped the King. One day a wise man came and gave the King a ring to which it had an inscription written on it saying, "<u>this too shall pass</u>." The King asked the wise man to explain these words and how it could possibly help him. The wise man explained that on days when he is feeling troubled, upset, or sad, that he is to read the words on the ring. The words on the ring would remind the King that his troubles and

sadness would pass. But the King also realized that the same phrase would also apply to times of prosperity and happiness. The King replied to the wise man saying that the words "this too shall pass" made him sad knowing that during prosperity and happiness, these things too would pass. So, he wandered how could the ring help him? The wise man replied that "yes it is true that even when we are feeling happy that it too shall pass but this ring is also a reminder to live in the present moment to fully experience every moment of life's joy and appreciate these times." [6]

We all want to feel happy and avoid suffering; we all want to feel good. What advice would you give to the king if you were asked? If Abby were the wise man, she would tell the king, "Don't worry; be happy." She would tell him that the more he can accept things, the easier life becomes. She would remind the king that grasping leads to monkeys being caught—or don't put your hand in a coconut because it's a trap.

The point is that by accepting, we can learn to let go and avoid analyzing how things should or shouldn't be to help us reach a state of peace. At times when we feel good, we can learn to appreciate the joy in whatever the experience is by connecting deeper through mindful awareness and presence in the moment. Or as Abby would say, "Let go of the coconut."

---

[6] Eckhart Tolle, A New Earth. Awakening to Your Life's Purpose (New York: Penguin Random House, 2016), 223–224.

Letting-Go Coconut Meditation

This letting-go coconut meditation will help you to become more aware of your thoughts and how to let go of them.

- Get into a comfortable position.
- With your eyes closed, begin slowly watching your mind.
    - Watching your mind means to picture yourself as if you are separated from your mind, as if you are watching a movie in front of you. The movie represents your thoughts that are generated from your mind. As your mind generates thoughts, be aware of them.
    - As the thoughts are generated, you can label the thoughts and call them *thinking* or *thoughts*. Labeling helps to gain some distance from the thoughts to help you become less attached to them. Because the mind is limitless, be aware that any thought is possible and can be generated. Be patient and kind with yourself. Keep resting the mind by watching and being aware of your thoughts. Notice without any judgment.
    - If your thoughts are coming in too fast, it's OK. Simply see these thoughts as a stream of thoughts or, better yet, like a river of thoughts. If you become agitated or frustrated, take a couple

of slow, deep breaths, focusing your attention on the breath. Take a slow breath in and an even slower breath out. Remember that you have absolutely no control over what thoughts come next into your mind. Similarly, like watching a movie, you have no control over what the movie will do next.
    - Do this for one to two minutes.
- Go back to the breath, and slowly breathe in and slowly breathe out, focusing your attention on the breath.
    - Do this for one to two minutes.
- Great work! Thank you for joining with me on this letting-go meditation.

The key is to practice every day until it becomes easier, as a set habit. Keep your practice short at the beginning, and repeat this several times throughout the day (e.g., the morning, the middle of the day, before you go to sleep, or whatever works best for you). In time, your thoughts will slow down, and your flooding river of thoughts will recede into a clear, slow-moving river of thoughts that come and go.

Dealing with Unpleasantry, Such as Frustration

Recall that in chapter 2, we compared the three levels of an experience to storytelling: level 1—the story; level 2—emotions; level 3—interoceptive awareness. What do you think were Abby's three levels, regarding the study room door being closed?

At level 1, Abby's story was something like this: "I can't believe these idiots don't know how to keep that damn door open. They know that it bothers me." At level 2, Abby would say, "I'm so f*cking mad." And finally, at level 3, if you asked Abby where it bothered her the most in her body, she would answer, "In my tummy."

Moving from level 1 to level 3, we shift our focus to our emotions to help us remove storytelling. At level 3 (interoceptive awareness), we start identifying our feelings in relation to the sensations generated within the body. When we talk about sensations, we are referring to either physical feelings or perceptions that we get when something happens or meets our bodies. Each of us feels frustration differently. Some might feel tension in the neck muscles. Others might feel tightness in the jaw. I usually feel it in my stomach.

It is important to bring awareness to the tension. Learning to recognize sensations in the body helps you to stop what you are doing, preventing any further harm, and then apply relaxation techniques to help you relax the tension (or stress). In addition, this also helps you to slow down your mind and remove storytelling.

Let's look at a specific meditation tool that can help bring interoceptive awareness and help bring relaxation to areas of tension. This meditation tool is called *sensory awareness focus*, or it can be called *sensory awareness meditation* (SAM). Sensory awareness meditation can be used not just for frustration but for many other emotions or emotional responses, such as anger, annoyance (disappointment, irritation), anxiety, craving, fear, sadness, shame, guilt, or worry. Here is how it works:

Sensory Awareness Meditation (SAM)

- Get comfortable and find a spot, either sitting or lying down or whatever position best suits you.
- Take a couple of slow, deep breaths.
    - Feel the air coming into your chest. Feel the expansion of your chest as the air comes in, and feel the decompression of your lungs as the air comes out.
- Shift your attention to belly breathing.
    - Try to make your belly round as you breathe in. When breathing out, force your belly or the belly button toward the spine.
    - Feel the sensation or the rise of the stomach and again the drop of the stomach.
- Take your index finger and your thumb, and slowly bring these two fingers together. Once you make a connection with the fingers, notice that sensation or the perception of skin-to-skin contact. Is it hot, warm, or cold? What does it feel like? Bring your awareness to that touch sensation. And now release the fingers slowly.
- Pick either your left or right arm, and bring it slowly toward your body so that your elbow starts to touch the side of your body. Feel that sensation.

- Put a little bit of pressure on it this time, and notice the difference between the initial contact and this additional pressure on the side. Notice if it's comfortable or not. Either way, notice without judgment. Let go, and let the arm rest and move it to the side again.
  - Bring your awareness back to the breath, and breathe slowly in and slowly out.
- Bring your feet together.
  - Slowly bring your feet together so that they touch each other. It could be either the toes touching or the sides of the feet. As you bring the feet together, notice the sensation of the touch or the perception of the feet touching. Notice the muscles contracting to make the feet come together. Hold for a moment and then let go. As you let go, feel the sensations of letting go, and feel what it's like to let the contraction of your muscles go. Feel the muscles relaxing as the tension subsides.
- Focus your attention on your face. Scrunch up your face, as if you are trying to tense up every muscle in your face. Hold it for a few seconds, and feel the tension. And now let go. Try it again. Did you notice the different sensations between holding and letting go? What did they feel like?
- Let's move down to the shoulders. Raise your shoulders slowly. As you raise your shoulders, hold for a couple of

seconds. Notice the feeling of the muscles contracting and the build-up of tension. Slowly lower your shoulders. Feel the difference between contracting your muscles and releasing them.
- Breathe in slowly, and hold your breath for a couple of seconds. And now let go. Try it again, but this time, bring your attention to what it feels like to hold your breath for a couple of seconds and the gentle release afterward. See and feel the difference between holding and letting go of your breath.
- Bring your attention to your body, and notice anything that arises (e.g., feeling the heart beating, hearing tummy sounds, feeling an itch, some type of discomfort). Try to focus your attention on whatever arises for a few seconds. If the feeling becomes too strong, then simply stop and go back to the breath.
- Finally, bring your awareness back on the breath. Breathe in and out slowly. As you breathe out say the word *ah* at the end. Notice how this makes you feel.
- Excellent work; you are done!

CHAPTER FOUR

Nourishing Happiness

ARE YOU READY TO BE HAPPY? SORRY, BUT THAT WAS A TRICK question. Being happy is not something you get or find. You can't find happiness like finding your socks in your drawer. If I say that I am looking for happiness, that means that I am looking for it somewhere outside of myself. See the dilemma? Yet we all spend so much time trying to find happiness. We look for it in a new job, a new car, a house. We say to ourselves that if only we could find the right person, then we would be happy. If we have children, then we truly will be happy.

OK, say you do find that Mr. or Mrs. Right. Or you get that new car that you have been dreaming about. What happens next? Do you stay in bliss? Will your mind now be happy? Will your mind now stop looking for happiness since you have achieved it? Think about the last time you wished for something to happen to make you happy. Once you got it, you were probably very happy. Now, think about how you feel today after you got what you wanted. Are you still in that state of happiness? After some time, did the happiness feeling go away?

Sometimes, I wish to have a house on the lake with lots of property, away from people. I imagine the tranquility of being away from the noise and bothersome people. We all are looking for happiness to help us get through our problems. We all feel the need to escape our problems, and we think that happiness is just around the corner. But that is not life. And that is not happiness. *Happiness is a state of mind in which you know, at this very moment, that you are complete.*

The problem we encounter is when we are not complete. We are not complete when we hunger for things that we do not have, instead of enjoying the things that we do have. We are not complete when we allow our thoughts, interpretations, and made-up stories to get in the way of happiness. We are not complete when we keep holding on to every offense that someone did or said. We are not complete when we are not connected with our true inner beings. The true inner being is a place where both mind and body are at peace. It is here, knowing that changing circumstances have no affect on happiness. When we are in this place, then we are grounded. Let me explain *being grounded* a little further.

To ground yourself means to be in the present moment, mindfully aware of your thoughts and actions, nonjudgmentally, and using your tools to return yourself to your natural self of peace and calmness. To ground yourself means that when you catch yourself going into habitual reactions, you stop yourself; instead of reacting, you respond appropriately with the knowledge, tools, and wisdom that you already have within you.

At times when I am meditating, I reach a state of peace, to which I refer as *happiness*. My state of happiness is grounded in the state of peace. Now, if I can *learn* to extend this state of happiness (peace) beyond meditation and into my day-to-day activities, then no matter what happens, I will be in a state of equanimity. My mind will be balanced or undisturbed by the experience of thoughts, emotions, and even pain. This is what is called being *enlightened*.

For happiness to extend beyond meditation and into day-to-day activities, it needs to be nourished. To ground yourself in happiness requires knowledge and practice. As Abby says, *You can't become a pianist by simply wishing and looking at pianos all day.* The same can be said about happiness. The tool of knowledge is continuous learning (to gain wisdom), while the tool of practice is mindfulness and meditation. Learning to combine both knowledge and practice helps to change our thinking process. When we change our thinking process, we form new brain cell connections (neuronal connections) to complement new thinking. It takes time to teach the brain newer thought patterns. Again, with knowledge, time, and practice, you will reinforce the state of happiness within yourself.

It might seem strange that to be happy, you need to practice it and even gain wisdom. Here is another way to look at it: Have you ever heard the cliché "stop and smell the roses"?

To appreciate a rose, you need knowledge and practice. You need knowledge in the form of understanding that a rose is beautiful, yet because of its thorns, it can hurt you if you don't handle it carefully. You need practice in the form of mindfulness to be fully present, to feel both appreciation and gratitude. Could you ever feel gratitude and appreciation for a rose if you've only seen it in a picture? Or if someone tried to describe what roses smell like? *Stop and smell the roses* implies that you focus your attention (be mindful in thoughts and actions) on the rose and use your sense perception of *smell* to appreciate its rich fragrance that words cannot express. If you want happiness, *stop* what you are doing, and mindfully see and "smell" what is going on in your mind and body, respectively. Then, respond appropriately to ground yourself; otherwise, unmindful thoughts and actions (or "thorns") can cause suffering to ourselves and others.

Tools to Nourish Happiness

Nourishing happiness in our day-to-day lives requires tools in our backpacks. These tools provide insight in how we think, what we say, and the actions that mirror our thoughts. These tools also help to improve us and our actions (e.g., interactions with others) to sustain happiness. And finally, they help to ground us into a more peaceful state. And remember, the more tools you have, the more you can nourish your happiness in your day.

Tool 1—Connect to Positive Energy

Positive energy is the active motion of the mind and body toward a state of happiness and peace. This movement comes from wishing that you and others would be happy and would avoid suffering. Moving the mind to this positive energy involves being connected to your true inner self, devoid of ego, resistance, and grasping. Positive energy for the body is defined in physical wellness. Basically, it means taking care of your body through healthy ways (e.g., eating healthily, exercising). When both the mind and body are connected to positive energy, we get a lifestyle that seeks gratitude, appreciation, optimism, and other desirable attributes.

To summarize, positive energy is not a thing that can be seen under the microscope; rather, it's a desire to think and do good. For example, sending someone *positive energy* is sending someone the desire or the wish for good things to help that person connect to happiness.

Connecting to positive energy is an active process. For your inner being, you connect with it through spiritual activities. Spiritual practice involves both actions and activities to bring about experiences and development toward peace, harmony, and finding purpose in life. There are many examples of spiritual practices: meditation, prayer, reflective time alone. Each practice involves spending time in yourself to become a better you.

Through reflection, we can see the areas of ourselves in which we want to improve. The more that we can transform ourselves for the better, the more we can give back to ourselves and others (we cannot give what we don't have). Spiritual practice is also connected to our bodies. For example, when we practice meditation, we learn to bring ourselves back to our calmer selves, which helps to decrease stress. When our stress is decreased, our overall health improves (hence, the mind/body connection).

There are other ways to connect to positive energy. Spend your time focusing on the positives throughout the day. Look for and talk to positive people. Try to learn as much as you can from people who can teach you about positive outlooks. Try to avoid negative people, and if you must be with negative persons, be mindful of your thoughts, words, and actions. Remember that you have the choice to walk away from the negative energy.

Avoid negativity in both giving and hearing negative comments. Go a day without listening to the news or other media. Try to watch movies or TV shows with a positive message. With more knowledge and tools (especially in mindfulness and meditation), you can change your thinking process to a more positive outlook.

If you find it hard to be positive, especially when you see and hear of all the violence, killing, diseases, and suffering on this planet, ask yourself this question: *Will any amount of worry or sadness change my or another person's situation?* A family member can be suffering from a disease, but it does no good—to you or to anyone—to worry about it. In fact, if you worry more, you create suffering for yourself and possibly for others. Remember that you can deal with your worry and anxiety through meditation by feeling the emotion (as previously discussed). Alternately, you can spend time using relaxation techniques to destress your mind and lower the stress hormones in your body. Dwelling on and worrying about the suffering in and around you will not change any situation or person, including your loved ones. Instead, remember that you want to feel good, no matter the situation, and when you feel good, you will suffer less and help more.

Tool 2—Seek Gratitude and Appreciation

Count your blessings. Be grateful for all that you have. Think about the people for whom you are grateful. Bring to mind all the people who have showed you love. Was it something as simple as someone calling you to see how you were doing? Was it a neighbor waving or saying hello? Recall someone who helped you in some way. Feel the gratitude for that person's love and kindness. Take some time to meditate on all the people who have helped you to get where you are today.

Can you feel grateful for being healthy, or being able to drink clean water, or enjoying a meal that some people do not have? When you stop, think, and look around you, you can find so many things to be grateful for. Take the time to write down all the things that you have in your life, and reflect upon them. If you still need some help with gratitude, look to nature. Look at the trees, and be grateful that they clean the air and give you oxygen to breathe. Think about all the different plants that not only give food but medicine as well.

Stop and smell the roses. Appreciate by recognizing all the good qualities in people or things. If you find it hard to see the good, remember that the mind inheritably tries to categorize things, people, and situations as good, bad, or neutral. However, things are never fixed, as situations can change, and something that was considered good can become bad. For example, a dispute with a good neighbor causes that person to become your enemy. The more you judge, the more you view things as good or bad.

As the Persian proverb says, "He who wants a rose must respect the thorn." Look past the thorn to appreciate the good qualities. What are some things you appreciate? What good qualities can you see in your neighbor or in the store clerk? How about the people with whom you are having difficulties? Can you recognize and appreciate a good quality? With a more positive outlook, you can lessen the degree that your mind wants to judge; you can learn see something "as is" and appreciate it.

Tool 3—Have No Expectations of Others

When you feel that someone owes you a favor for something you did for him or her, you are relying on an expectation that is based on "I help you, and you help me." If that expectation is not fulfilled, it can lead to your feelings being hurt for a variety reasons: (1) feeling that the person does not care for you; (2) feeling that the person does not appreciate your time and effort; or (3) feeling that the expectation itself (I help you, and you help me) was not fulfilled.

Say, for example, that you do something nice for someone, with the expectation that one day that person will reciprocate the favor. Tomorrow comes along, but that person does not return the favor. How would you feel? Hurt? Betrayed? At this point, your mind will harbor resentment toward the person, which will lead to hurt feelings. If you see this person in the future, you might feel hurt and say hurtful things, which can lead to more suffering. Within families, especially, there is a strong expectation that each person *must* help the other. How can you *not* have that expectation of a family member when things need to get done?

Instead of expecting that your wishes will be taken care of, why not communicate to the person that you need help? If you need help in washing the dishes from your kids or your spouse, you need ask (and maybe explain why). Otherwise, if you expect your kids to wash the dishes every night, you likely will be disappointed. If you feel that you should not have to ask because you are a parent, spouse, or friend, then this will lead to suffering in both ego identification and expectation. Try to be honest with yourself, and look at the reason(s) why it might be difficult for you to ask for help (e.g., embarrassment or pride). Be mindful of your reluctance to ask for help, and meditate on the feelings generated so that you can be in a calmer state. With a clear mind, it will be easier to ask for help without your mind resisting.

You can learn to be mindful of not having expectations of others. It will help to remind yourself daily by repeating this affirmation: "I will not have any expectations of others." When thoughts or feelings arise from disappointed expectations, deal with your feelings first through meditation, and then move on to the above affirmation. The fewer expectations you have, the more peaceful or happier you will be.

> Then Jesus said to his host, "When you give a luncheon or dinner, do not invite your friends, your brothers or sisters, your relatives, or your rich neighbors; if you do, they may invite you back and so you will be repaid. But when you give a banquet, invite the poor, the crippled, the lame, the blind, and you will be blessed. Although they cannot repay you, you will be repaid at the resurrection of the righteous." (Luke 14:12–14 NIV)

Jesus gives us guidance to give freely without expectations, which will ultimately lead to happiness. This happiness comes from the transformation of the inner self in recognizing that giving without expectations, including not expecting something in return, leads to a profound inner joy.

Tool 4—Be Mindful of Blame

When something goes wrong, our minds look for blame. When a fault occurs, we look to blame others or things. If we are at work when a mistake occurs, employees will blame each other or a supervisor will blame a worker. Parents accuse each other if their child has done something wrong, or they blame the child. Why do our minds need to blame? It begins by understanding the negative emotions that get created when something goes wrong. When anger, frustration, judgment, or hatred arise, our minds do not know how to deal with this negative energy.

Becoming mindful in recognizing the mind's irritation can help you to stop the mind from reacting to the negative emotion and stop you from either blaming yourself or someone else. Look at it logically: could a situation change or be reversed if you were to blame? No amount of blame will change anything that has already occurred. Instead, the blame will only make the situation worse and cause greater suffering to you and to others.

Training your mind not to react to blame is very difficult. You can learn, however, that when negative emotions arise, you can take positive steps to deal with the irritation. Begin by slowing things down—take a couple of slow, deep breaths to calm the mind. It's important to go as slowly as you can, especially on the out breath, to help you to relax more. Once the negative emotions begin to lessen, you will be able to look at the situation with more clarity and respond appropriately to the situation.

Always remember that the mind is looking for blame to rationalize the irritation. It's a form of automatic reaction that the mind wants to express the negative emotions. With patience, practice, and loving-kindness toward yourself, you will recognize the blame reaction and, ultimately, learn not to respond outwardly but respond inwardly by dealing with the negative feelings. When you look to nature, the flower does not blame the wind for losing its petals; instead, the petals simply fall.

Tool 5—Be Happy for Others

Two neighbors each had a son. One day, the first neighbor told the second neighbor that his son had been accepted to medical school.

The second neighbor responded, "That's great. I too have some news to share; my son has been accepted to law school."

The first neighbor responded, "That's great, but my son finished with honors. He's sure to be a top-notch surgeon one day."

The second neighbor said, "My son also finished with high honors, and I'm sure that he will be a great lawyer."

Neither neighbor could be happy for the other. Each neighbor needed to compare himself to the other. If one neighbor had simply acknowledged the good news and was happy for the other neighbor, he would be able to feel joy for the good news that was being shared.

Two friends were walking down their street, and one friend noticed that a neighbor had purchased a brand-new expensive car. The friend approached the neighbor and complimented him on how beautiful the car looked.

The neighbor responded graciously. "Yes, I'm very happy," and he explained that the car was expensive, and he mentioned all the features that came with it.

The friend again acknowledged the beauty of the car.

In this story, we see once again that when we compliment or are happy for someone without any story behind it, we can truly appreciate and share in the good fortune that the person has experienced. If, on the other hand, we simply want to compare ourselves to others, then this will lead to suffering.

We suffer because when we can't see the joy that our friend has experienced, we internalize and either judge or compare ourselves to the friend, which again leads to suffering. The mind—specifically, the ego—tends to recognize the inadequacies that we might have when compared to someone's good fortune. The ego looks to fulfill its need of self-recognition, instead of recognizing the joy that good fortune brings. By simply being happy for someone's good fortune, you share in the enjoyment it offers.

Tool 6—Counterconditioning Meditation

In counterconditioning meditation, you use visualization to generate an emotional response to replace a negative emotion with a positive emotion. This tool helps you to replace your negative thoughts with happiness. Here is how it works:

- Get comfortable; find a spot either sitting or lying down or whatever position suits you best.
- Take a couple of slow, deep breaths. Repeat this a few times.

- Bring to your mind a past situation that has made you happy. For example, it could be receiving a long hug from a family member or a friend; enjoying a good book; walking through nature; enjoying working in your garden; playing with or holding your pet.
    - Visualize how it made you feel.
    - Focus on the emotions that it generated.
    - Once you feel the emotions, try to breathe them in. *Breathing them in* simply means you try to feel the emotion and breathe into that emotion.
    - If you feel that the emotion is somewhere outside of you, visualize this positive emotion entering your body by breathing it in.
    - Essentially, what we're trying to do is store this positive emotion into the brain or mind. We want to store good things—things that make us feel happy, joyful, and peaceful.
- Bring to your mind a situation that you have dealt with in the past that generated strong emotions. For example, it could be rejection, judgment, criticism, anger, or jealousy. It could be a situation where someone did or said something to you that made you feel hurt or resentful.
    - Note: If thinking about it generates a lot of deep feelings and this becomes difficult, then *stop*. Instead, go back to visualizing and breathing in the positive, peaceful, and joyful situation.
- As you're visualizing this negative situation, without going too deeply into it (just like touching the surface of

water without jumping into it), recall how the situation felt.

- o Once you sense this negative energy or negative feelings/emotions, go back to the first visualization of the positive situation that generated positive emotions.
- Take those positive feelings or emotions and visualize them as if they form a cover. For example, it could be a blanket, carpet, or pillow. As you're visualizing these positive energies in the form of a cover, go back and visualize the negative situation, and drop the cover on the negative energy. Visualize the negative emotions being covered and being replaced by positive energy.
  - o If the negative emotions start creeping back, go back to visualizing the positive energy, and once again, drop and cover up the negative energy.
    - Note: If this becomes too difficult, *stop* and go back to breathing; notice your breath breathing in slowly and breathing out slowly. Go back to the positive emotions, and stay there, feeling them once again.
- Finally, bring your attention back on the breath, slowly breathing in and slowly breathing out. Do this a few more times.
- Excellent! You are done.

CHAPTER FIVE

We Need to Be Kind to Ourselves Because It Is Not Entirely Our Fault

OUR MINDS HAVE AN AFFINITY FOR GENERATING NEGATIVE STUFF, as well as holding and storing that stuff. When things go wrong, our minds generate blaming thoughts and self-criticism. And even when things go right, our minds still can generate negative thinking, such as, "I don't deserve to be happy," "I should feel guilty about this," or "I'm not a good person."

To complicate things, past events that trigger negative thinking and feelings can get stored in the brain. For example, past guilt and resentment can get triggered again by associated thoughts and feelings. Just the thought of guilt can trigger a guilty memory. Similarly, hearing a person's name can trigger a resentment that happened back in our childhoods. Our minds are fixated on the negatives. We could be talking to a friend, for example, and that friend could say ten positive things about us and only one negative thing. Yet at the end of the day, the only thing we remember is that one negative comment. In addition, our minds, of their own accord, move into and out of past and future thinking, all within seconds. Our minds have a hard time sitting in the present moment. With all that moving around, the mind can generate a lot of negative stuff in the form of past and future worries. This is why it is *not entirely our fault* that we think the way we do. Our minds have been programed this way. But there is hope—hope in the form of *kindness*. Let's start with our self-criticism example: Our minds inherently like to blame or criticize, especially the self. Sometimes, we might say to ourselves that self-criticism helps to motivate us to improve. Does being harsh on ourselves really work?

Try to remember when you were in school, and you felt good about something you did. Most likely, it was because a teacher, a coach, or a friend encouraged you with kind words that motivated you to keep trying. You then were able to get through your specific challenge and emerge on the other side feeling accomplished and with good feelings. You may have had doubt and self-criticism, but through positive reinforcement, encouragement, motivation, and a few kind words, you got the energy needed to overcome your challenge.

Likewise, overcoming self-criticism is also handled through kindness toward oneself. So in this example, we overcome the negative self-criticism that our minds like to do through being kind to ourselves. Let me ask you this question: Can you overcome fear and worry with more fear and worry? If your answer is no, then the same logic follows that you cannot overcome negative thinking by using more negative thinking. If I criticize myself—"What is wrong with me? I'm such a loser?"—this thinking won't be solved by using more self-criticism. I need tools to help change the negative thoughts to positive thinking. That is why we use counterconditioning meditation to generate positive thoughts to overcome negative thinking. Similarly, using positive affirmations in the form of repeating kind words to ourselves is another example of using good thoughts to help create positive changes in our brains. Using tools like counterconditioning and positive affirmations help reinforce the brain to store good stuff (positive thinking) and ultimately change our neuronal connections to create new thinking patterns.

I mentioned that our minds like to jump from past to future, which also contributes to that negative stuff that gets generated. How does being kind to ourselves help with this? I've heard of the mind described as a puppy. To train a puppy requires patience, understanding, positive reinforcement, and kindness. When the puppy does something right, we give it a treat to help motivate the desired behavior. Our minds require the same when dealing with unwanted stuff, like negative thoughts and emotions.

Helping the puppy to sit requires training and kindness, just like your mind. When you feel yourself thinking about and feeling past events or worrying about something in the future, try to see these thoughts and emotions as simply a "puppy mind." Visualize your mind as a puppy wanting to play, jump, and run—basically always in motion. Getting the puppy mind to sit requires grounding yourself through various tools (e.g., breathing, meditation, yoga). Yelling at the puppy to sit does not work. Similarly, self-criticism and demanding that the mind be still also does not work. But when you are kind to yourself, you open your understanding that the mind likes to move freely into the past and future and has difficulty sitting still in the present. Again, with kindness, use meditation and mindfulness to help the mind sit still by observing any negative thoughts without judgment and responding with gentleness, that this too shall pass.

And now here is an Abby story to reinforce what I have said so far: Abby always has been kind to herself. When she feels hungry, she eats. When she wants to take a nap, she does. There is never any judgment or self-criticism in anything she decides to do. In her human voice, she would say things like, "I deserve to sleep on the sofa today," "I need someone to pet me," or "I deserve love." One day, I was looking for her in the basement and found her lying down near her litter box. It did not bother her to sit so close to the smelly box. There was no embarrassment or shame in what she was doing. In her mind, she was simply enjoying the moment without judgment. Whatever Abby does, she does it with gentleness toward herself without the negative talk. Abby accepts who she is without self-criticism.

Ways to be Kind to Yourself

1. Accept Yourself!

Nick Keomahavong, a Buddhist monk, tells this story: One day, a rose was planted in a desert. The rose became alive, started to look around, and noticed all the cacti growing around it. The rose said to itself, "These cacti are very strong and sturdy. I love the thorns and how tough they are, as they can endure the desert heat. I like their resiliency because they don't need much water. They are truly amazing." The rose spent much time comparing itself to the cacti, wishing it too was a cactus. One day, the rose decided to see a therapist to see if the therapist could help it become a cactus. The therapist gave the rose many coping skills and other tools for how to be like a cactus. After years of struggle, the rose was not happy because it still could not become like a cactus. The rose finally said, "I wish someone had told me to take the time to realize who I am by design. There is nothing wrong with being either a rose or a cactus. That is just the nature of who we are".[7]

I love this story of self-acceptance. Many times, we find ourselves wishing to be someone else. We think that if we surround ourselves with people who we want to become that we will somehow change into them. But this does not happen; rather, it results in suffering. If we want to connect to our true

---

[7] "What I Wish My Therapist Told Me: A Buddhist Monk's Reflection," https://www.youtube.com/watch?v=SysctKGdOKA, accessed 11/8/21.

inner selves, then we need to be devoid of ego, resistance, and grasping. Training our minds not to react to ego, resistance, and grasping takes time and practice. *Anything on which we want to improve takes a lot of time and practice.*

Take the time to connect to your true self. Reflect using your tools of mindfulness and meditation to help you discover your true nature. Don't try to become someone you are not. At this very moment, you and I are imperfect, and that is perfect enough for us to accept ourselves for who we really are. This does not mean that you should not try to improve who you are; it means you should accept and love who you are. Look inside and see all the good qualities that you like about yourself. Make a list, or better yet, start a journal and write down all the positive things about yourself. Keep in mind that this list or journal is about your inner qualities. You are trying to get to the core of your true inner self.

Next, try to connect your beautiful qualities to get a sense of who you are. Say, for example, you like taking long walks, hiking, and reading books. In addition, you feel more comfortable talking with one person rather than a group of people. In this example, you might see yourself as an introvert. With this in mind, you can nurture yourself by looking for things that seem fitting to your character. Maybe a career in counseling in a one-to-one interaction setting is in line with your nature. By learning to accept yourself and nurturing your strengths in the context of your environment, you can become a better you, like a rose in a garden.

2. Who Cares What Others Think or Say?

I like to spend quiet prayer/meditation time in the mornings. A reflective phrase I say to myself is, "May I not care what others think or say." What I am really saying is, may I be gentle with myself when someone criticizes me. Through gentleness, I learn to put aside the opinions of others and recognize that who I am is imperfect, and that is perfect enough. And when I do get offended by someone's opinion or remark, I ask myself, "Am I hurt because of my ego?" Knowing that my ego has gotten a blow helps me to separate the real me from my ego. The real me is a place where my mind is still and undisturbed by opinions. But the real me still needs to deal with my mind to get me back to the place of tranquility.

When my thoughts and emotions are ruminating on what someone said, then I remind myself that it is *my* opinion of myself that is important. I still need to deal with all those ruminating thoughts and emotions, however, and to do this, I try to be gentle with myself. I give myself kindness and compassion as I work on my hurt feelings. Over time, it does become easier to deal with my hurt feelings. Instead of brooding over several days, it might take me only one day.

This is why it's necessary to keep working on myself, in terms of learning as much as I can (e.g., understanding the ego) and maintaining a daily meditation practice. I do find myself wishing to be a cactus, resilient to the opinions of others, but that is not who I am, and that is OK. Gentleness comes in the form of compassion, to treat myself with love and acceptance for feeling the way I do. Being gentle means knowing that my opinion of myself is more important than what others think or say.

I once heard someone say that there is a way not to get hurt from someone's opinion. Simply remember that a fact is a fact, and there is no need to argue against it. If you accept a fact, then how can you dispute it or feel hurt that someone stated a fact? For example, someone saying that I am becoming bald is a fact. My hair is thinning, and, most likely, the top of my head will one day be bald. The remark may be unkind, but the truth is that my hair is thinning. If I can accept this fact, then there's no reason to get offended.

But if someone says something ridiculous to you, why get offended? If the sun is shining, and someone says it's raining, their comment is incorrect. If they are incorrect, then why get offended? Again, there's no reason to get hurt by something that is inaccurate and ridiculous. Ask yourself if it's your ego that has been offended. If yes, then be gentle and kind to yourself, and recognize that you are not your ego. You are not your thoughts and emotions, and as such, be mindful to help you see the real you versus your ego. The real you is the rose, living your life based on your opinion of yourself, devoid of someone else's standards, thinking, or belief. I encourage you to start today by saying to yourself, "May I not care what others think or say."

3. Sometimes, They Are Not Your Chickens

My grandparents had a barn that had cows as well as chickens. My grandmother would ask me to gather the chickens into the barn at the end of the day—and I would become exhausted from chasing chickens. I think the chickens knew they needed to go back into the barn, but they just wanted to have some fun with the new guy!

Chasing chickens is like trying to take care of yourself without knowing how to do it. You need to take care of yourself first. You may think this is selfish, but, in fact, you are taking care of yourself so that you can be of service to others. You can't give what you don't have. You are building your inner-strength muscles so that when the time comes, you will be ready to help. In addition, if you spread yourself thin, not only will you harm yourself, but you will not be able to help others properly. Take care of yourself. Take care of your chickens first. When you are ready with the proper internal resources, not only will you be able to take care of your chickens, but you will be able to take care of other people's chickens.

Plus, sometimes they are not your chickens. You can't help everyone because not everyone is ready to be helped. Sometimes, they are not your chickens to take care of. Only when the student is ready does the teacher appear. Have you ever tried to help someone to stop drinking, smoking, or any other unhealthy habit? All the help and advice you give an alcoholic won't help that person to change. Change, as we know, must come from the inside. Yes, we can support and offer help when asked or needed. But there will be a time when you must realize that you cannot keep trying to help because you will burn yourself down.

Sometimes they are not your chickens. Be kind to yourself by removing any guilt you might feel for situations that you are not ready to handle or cannot handle. It is important to work on yourself to be the best you can be.

4. Warming the Heart Affirmation

Step 1: Close your eyes and slowly watch your mind to give your mind a rest.

- Watch your thoughts that are generated from your mind, and be aware of them.
- Keep resting the mind by watching and being aware of your thoughts. Notice without any judgment.

Step 2: Take in slow, deep breaths; do this for a couple of minutes to help gain focus.

Step 3: Repeat the following phrase several times, and try to feel the generosity toward yourself: "May I be happy. May I avoid suffering. May I avoid the causes of suffering."

Step 4: Repeat the following phrase several times, and try to feel the affection or warmth toward yourself: "May I be kind and compassionate toward myself."

5. Give Yourself as Much Time as Needed to Heal at Your Own Pace

One day, we wake up feeling great, and the next day, we feel blue or just not ourselves. Throughout the course of the day, we could go through many ups and downs, but some *downs* tend to hold on to us for a long time. For example, feeling down after the death of a loved one can last a lifetime. During these difficult times, we may experience strong feelings and emotions. Our minds might find it hard to focus, as our thoughts seem scattered or unclear. Using meditation, we feel the emotions that are generated from the suffering, and through mindfulness, we learn how to view and deal with them in a nonjudgmental way. Viewing the down thoughts and emotions without putting a name, a story, or blame to them helps to lessen the negative energy. Eventually, a sense of peace ensues.

When we practice mindfulness and meditation at times of suffering, the mind can find its way to peace. It is important to give ourselves as much time as we need to heal at our own pace, rather than what others expect. We all deal with our "down" in different ways, and we all heal at different rates. Remember that a rose and cactus need different amounts of water; similarly, the time needed to deal with the "downs" differs from person to person.

Allow yourself the time to deal with your emotions and feelings, especially those that seem to resurface. Be mindful to seek additional support systems when you need them (e.g., talking to family or a close friend, counseling, seeing your family doctor). The more tools you have, the more solutions you have. You might try using meditation and mindfulness apps to help you find the specific guided meditations that you need. Be kind and patient with yourself, and peace will find its way back into your mind. Over time, strong emotions and thoughts will slowly diminish.

6. You Have the Choice to Walk Away

I keep hearing a couple of phrases with regard to dealing with people: "This job would be great if it wasn't for the people," and "You can choose your friends, but you can't choose your family." Seems that many difficult people are found at work, and we often can't choose with whom we work. Likewise, we can't choose specific family members—parents, siblings, and other relatives. When we remove all the difficult people, we are left with friends. And regarding friends, "A good friend is hard to find." These three phrases may give the impression that people, in general, are difficult and that the only people we like are our one or two good friends (if we find them). I define a *difficult person* as someone who is unmindful or unaware of what he or she is thinking and saying, which causes causing suffering to that person and/or others.

What does "Ways to Be Kind to Yourself" have to do with dealing with difficult people? Being kind to yourself means that you have the freedom to walk away from difficult people when they are being *unmindful*. You don't have to stand in the middle of the road, waiting to get hit by a drunk driver who is swerving everywhere with no control in he is doing. Instead, you have the freedom to step aside to avoid collision.

If someone is being mean to you on the phone, you can say, "I don't want to deal with your unpleasantry. When you can calm down, then you I'll be willing to talk to you further." Then hang up the phone. Being kind to yourself means that you don't allow yourself to be a punching bag; you don't allow coworkers to say harsh things to you. You can respond by saying that you don't appreciate their harsh words and then walk away. *Walking away* gives you the time to ground yourself. Walking away gives you that pause to do deep breathing and to collect your thoughts.

When dealing with difficult people, your emotions and thoughts can become strong, which, in turn, can cloud your judgment and lead to unmindful words and actions. Getting some space helps you to gain clarity. If you can't walk away from a difficult person, for whatever reason, be mindful of your thoughts and emotions. Try to focus on your breath to help calm you. When choosing to walk away, remember to deal with your own feelings afterward, as built-up energy (e.g., adrenaline) can still linger, and you want to be able to bring yourself back to peace.

Summary

We started this chapter understanding that it is not entirely our fault why we think and feel certain ways; that is how we were programmed. Rewiring or changing our thinking

We Need to Be Kind to Ourselves Because It Is Not Entirely Our Fault

requires training. Training the mind is like training a puppy. The puppy needs kindness, gentleness, and patience. Similarly, our puppy minds also need these same qualities to retrain our thinking. Positive reinforcement and a positive attitude toward ourselves are necessary to create change. Learning first to accept ourselves with a positive attitude allows us to nurture and strengthen our inner nature and allows us to accept both our strengths and weaknesses.

We can work on ourselves to be the best we can be by using counterconditioning and positive affirmations to help reinforce positive thinking. Putting our opinions of who we are above the opinions of others will help to build our inner qualities. And when we reach certain roadblocks, it is OK to take the time necessary to heal at our own pace and to accept our limitations of being of service to others. We need to take care of ourselves first to be able to help others. And when we encounter difficult situations that we are not ready to handle, we must accept our feelings and know that this is natural and OK. (As I said earlier, *sometimes they aren't your chickens*).

Finally, with difficult situations come difficult people. Remember that you have the choice to walk away when dealing with difficult people. Walking away simply means that you are trying to gain some space to help you to ground yourself and to bring yourself back to peace.

CHAPTER SIX

Spiritual Wellness and Happiness

SPIRITUAL WELLNESS AND HAPPINESS ARE LINKED, AS BOTH ARE grounded in inner peace. Spiritual wellness is the pursuit of the meaning and purpose of life, while striving for a state of peace with oneself and others. In spiritual wellness, we can use *spiritual practice* to help us strive for or obtain a state of peace. Spiritual practice involves both actions and activities to bring about experiences and development toward peace and inner calm.

Both spiritual wellness and spiritual practice follow the same path toward peace, harmony, and finding purpose in life. There are many spiritual practices (e.g., meditation, prayer, reflective time), and each complement spiritual wellness. In meditation, we learn to accept and let go of our thoughts and emotions to provide space for the mind to free itself from disturbances; then the mind can find its way back to inner peace. In essence, meditation is a spiritual practice that helps bring about inner calmness by accepting experiences as they are. When we practice meditation, we develop our spiritual wellness. Developing our spiritual wellness strengthens our happiness on a mental level.

Spiritual wellness connects us with life's purpose and meaning. It may seem that we all carry a different purpose and meaning, but ultimately, we all want to be happy and avoid suffering. Spiritual wellness, like happiness, is grounded in inner peace. Our inner peace resides in the inner dimension of our well-being, rather than the outer (physical or material things). The word *spiritual* relates to the human spirit or soul, which again describes the inner dimension of our being. Developing and having a deeper understanding of spiritual wellness strengthens our happiness because we see that the connection of long-lasting happiness is on the mental level and not on the physical level. When we can shift our focus on the inner dimension, we can then experience a deeper and more profound level of happiness. Understanding our inner self helps us to see who we are, which can dramatically impact our happiness.

Try this simple activity:

1. Answer this question: "Who are you?"
2. Answer these questions: "How complete are you? Why?"

Each question above is related to the other, and they gauge the level of happiness in your life. Let me explain:

"Who are you?" You could answer this question by giving your first and last name, followed by a description of things you like and don't like. You could answer by describing your occupation or that you are a mother or father of two children. You could answer with a physical description of who you are, along with your place of birth and nationality. All these answers describe things that can change. You can change your first name. Does this mean you are no longer who you are? You can change your occupation, number of children, and your physical identity. Even your place of birth can change. For example, if you were born in the former Yugoslavia, the name of your new place of birth would have changed (e.g., Croatia, Bosnia). *Who* you are can change, depending on the answer you give. Defining who you are by external things can change your happiness.

"How complete are you?" How did you answer this question? Some people say that they feel complete because their lives are good. Others could say, "If only I had two children, then my life would be complete," or "If my job was better, I would feel more complete." Once again, the level of completeness can change, depending on outside factors. If I get a fulfilling job, a new car, a house, a new relationship, two kids, etc., then I will be complete. As you can see, the list can go on forever, and the level of completeness will never be complete. Defining *how* complete you are by external things can also change your happiness level.

If your answer to "Who are you?" does not change over time or is not dependent upon circumstances, then knowing yourself or knowing who you are is a constant. "How complete are you?" If your answer to this question produces a constant—it doesn't change depending on things or circumstances—then your answer would always be, "I am complete." Therefore, if who you are and your level of completeness is a constant, then your state of peace is grounded, regardless of what happens. This is called being *enlightened.* Finding these constants is what spiritual wellness is about.

Spiritual wellness connects us to our human spirits or souls, which is not linked to the outer physical dimension and does not change. When our happiness is defined or linked to our inner dimension, then it too does not change. If we link our human spirits or souls to our happiness, then this becomes a constant.

Happiness is being in a state of peace and knowing, at this very moment, that you are complete and that you are a spiritual being.

This definition of happiness is grounded in the state of peace, regardless of what happens. A person would be in a state of equanimity, as his or her mind is balanced or undisturbed by the experience of thoughts, emotions, or pain. The words *this very moment* describe the present moment. In this present moment, we are not thinking about the past or the future. We are not resisting, comparing, or grasping; instead, we are accepting without judgment. In this definition of happiness, the words *knowing that you are complete* mean that your completeness is a constant (not changing due to things or circumstances). And who you are is a spiritual being, which also does not change or is not dependent on the physical dimension (things or circumstances).

Therefore, I am a spiritual being, and a spiritual being never changes; my level of completeness is complete. My definition of who I am is always the same because I am a spiritual being. Because I am a spiritual being, I know who I am, and therefore I know myself. Thus, I am complete.

Spiritual Being

Once there were two friends who had known each other since elementary school. They grew up in the same neighborhood and attended the same high school. At the time of their graduation, one friend decided to pursue studies in theology at a faraway university overseas. The other enrolled in science at a nearby university. After many years apart, as each was near the completion of his studies, they decided to get together.

The theology friend said that he'd decided to become a priest because he felt a presence or a calling. He described this presence as falling in love. "When you fall in love, you just know it. You feel it. You know that this is the person with whom you want to spend the rest of your life." The theology friend was sure that his friend would try to dispel this presence or calling as nonfactual and nonscientific.

To his surprise, however, his friend responded, "When I started to study physics and biology, I gained remarkable knowledge in understanding how things work and what they are made up of. Everything seemed in order. As my studies continued, I realized that when you break down a human being into its smallest parts (cells, molecules, atoms), the sum of these parts do not equal the whole. Combining parts together does not explain, for example, love. There is no love molecule, and even if you did find one and broke it down into smaller parts, to the last possible particle, the sum of these particles would not equal love or explain love. This means that there is something more out there than just particles."

Two friends coming together from two different paths in life both described spiritual wellness. One friend felt meaning in his life, while the other saw more to life than just molecules. In spiritual wellness we can uncover a greater depth of knowledge in understanding the self to avoid unnecessary suffering and ultimately to be happy. The more we are tuned in with our inner dimension, the greater the connection of consciousness or awareness to our inner being/spirit/soul, and this strengthens happiness on a mental level.

Learning to listen to our inner spirit begins with quieting the mind. In the vast resources that I have encountered, the main theme that keeps resurfacing is that of mindfulness and meditation as the tools needed to become enlightened or fully aware. You are a spiritual being! We are all spiritual beings. This does not change. The only thing that can change is your level of awareness to your being.

How Aware Are You of Your Self? Reflection

When the mind is at peace, we can learn to see our inner dimension. We use meditation to help quiet the mind. We use reflection to see areas of ourselves that we want to improve or learn to become a better person. In learning how to be a better person, you will help avoid unnecessary suffering to both you and others.

What is *reflection*? Reflection is thinking about your thoughts and emotions and how they might or might not serve you better. Reflection is spending some alone time with yourself. You are not judging or beating yourself up; instead, you are trying to see if you can look for better ways to bring about happiness and less suffering. Try this reflection activity:

Step 1: Find a quiet place.

Step 2: Breathe in slowly and breathe out slowly. Do this for a couple of minutes to help gain focus.

Step 3: Ask yourself, without judgment or criticism, as if you are asking a good friend, "What areas of my behavior would I like to improve?" Here are some examples:

- More patience
- Better communication
    - Less gossiping

- - Better listening
  - Less interrupting or talking over others
- Better temperament
- Less guilt on yourself or on others
- Less ego (e.g., the need to be right all the time)
- Less insecurity (e.g., jealousy)

Step 4: If it helps, write down the things on which you want to improve so that it takes them off your mind and places them onto a paper; that will help you to look at it more objectively and with less judgment.

Step 5: Remind yourself of the following: It is not entirely your fault as to why you think, feel, and behave certain ways because that is how you were programmed. To rewire or change your thinking requires training. Training the mind is like training a puppy. The puppy needs kindness, gentleness, and patience. Be kind, gentle, and patient with yourself.

Step 6: End by taking a couple of slow breaths.

Learning to reflect, as with any other skill, takes time, practice, and knowledge. Here is an example in the reflection process: Say you are having a bad day, and in the evening, you decide to do some meditation to help calm down your mind and body. You decide to reflect on the day, and you ask yourself what went wrong and what went well (e.g., could you have responded versus reacting?). While you are reflecting you catch yourself judging and criticizing yourself. With kindness and compassion, you say to yourself, "It's OK," and you keep repeating these words to settle the mind. As you are reflecting, you realize that at one point in the day, you lost your temper. Now you ask yourself, "Why did I lose my temper?" At first, you say that it was your spouse's fault for making you lose your temper. As you watch your thoughts, you become aware of blame. You think back to something you once heard: "When something goes wrong, our minds look for blame." You remember that blame occurs when the mind is not able to handle negative emotions.

Once again, you ask yourself, "What was I feeling that caused me to lose my temper?" You recall you felt frustrated because you were pressed for time, trying to do a million things. And at the time, the babysitter called and was unavailable to help that day. You realize that the reason you were frustrated was that things did not go as expected. You pick up on the word *expected* and think back on something that you read: "When things do not go our way and our expectations are not met, we get hurtfully disappointed. With great expectations come great hurt." So now you ask yourself, "What can I do to improve?" Reflecting on the solutions, you write them down:

- When I notice myself feeling frustrated, I will take a couple of slow, deep breaths. This will help to calm me down, and I will become more of aware of the present moment so that my mind is not racing.

- I noticed that my neck muscles are somewhat tight and sore. I think that when I get frustrated, I tighten them and cause this muscle tension.
    - I need to explore SAM—sensory awareness meditation—to help me recognize when I am tensing my neck muscles.
    - SAM can also help me to apply relaxation techniques to help me relax the tension in my neck.
- I need to find at least ten minutes in the day to meditate (SAM). Early mornings seem like a good time to meditate.
- I am going to start tomorrow.

The above example shows how knowledge and practice come together to help us become better through reflecting in areas of ourselves that we want to improve, to unlock happiness and avoid unnecessary suffering.

Greater Awareness of Ourselves through Prayer

Our level of awareness to our beings can change. The greater the awareness, the closer we get to who we really are. The closer we get, the greater the power in sustaining happiness and avoiding suffering.

Prayer is a spiritual practice, the path of which helps to bring peace and stillness. When we pray, we bring a greater awareness of ourselves and of others. For example, prayer helps us to seek and ask for help with the struggles that we encounter. And because our minds are not perfect, praying helps us to see the inner struggles that we all share. The twelve steps of Alcoholics Anonymous are used to help individuals with their spiritual and mental health: to be mindful of thoughts and of negative and self-defeating attitudes and behaviors; bettering oneself; and being grateful. When we talk to God (or to a higher power or to the universe), we become aware of our thoughts, emotions, fears, worries, doubts, hopes, and desires. This awareness can help bring about change in areas that we want to improve.

Prayer is a connection between becoming aware and seeking improvement. For example, when we become irritated, we can pray instead of reacting. Prayer opens our minds to see our irritation and become aware of it. Prayer helps us to seek improvement by talking to God and asking for help to deal with the irritation to improve our peace of mind. When we are irritated, what are we asking God for? We could ask for tolerance, patience, and kindness toward ourselves for the irritation. Will God deliver all our requests?

There is a story of a man who was stuck on his roof because there was a great flood all around him. As the water slowly started to rise, he prayed to God, asking to be saved. While he was praying, a man came by in a rowboat and offered to help the man on the roof. But the man ignored him and continued to pray. The water rose even higher. A speedboat came by, and the people in the boat yelled at the man to climb down into the boat with them. But the man ignored them. The water rose even higher, and now the man was standing on the roof as the water rose to his chest. A rescue helicopter came by and dropped a rope for the man to climb up. But again, the man refused, saying he was waiting for God to rescue him. Eventually, the water rose higher, and the man drowned. When the man reached heaven, he asked God, "Why didn't you save me?" God responded, "I sent you a rowboat, a speedboat, and finally a helicopter. What more did you want?"

Waiting for God's help can come in different forms. If we close our minds to the possibilities, then, just like the old man on the roof, we will never look for or be ready when help comes. Opening our minds means discarding our egos, fears, and worries and being open to accepting new ideas, knowledge, and skills. When we pray, we create the space for self-improvement (self-change) by listening with an open mind to the answers that unfold when we are ready to accept them.

When we need help to change, prayer can be a guiding force to help us seek and allow God (the universe) to answer. Just like the famous phrase says: when the student is ready, the teacher will appear.

Three Steps to Help You with Self-Change

Step 1: Pick Your Meditation

My cat, Abby, is a very good meditator—she uses different types of meditation to help with her needs. There is the *easy sleep meditation*, where she uses relaxation techniques to fall asleep. She is very good at this one because in one moment, she is awake, and a minute later, she is asleep. When she's outside on the deck, which backs onto a ravine area, she uses what I call *attention to external sensory stimuli meditation*. This type of meditation is when she focuses all her attention on external stimuli (also known as birds). Next comes *being in the present moment meditation*. This is the one where she has her eyes half closed and allows whatever is happening around her to simply happen. This she does when we are watching TV, and she is sitting on the couch with us. And I think her favorite meditation is the one called *joy meditation*. In joy meditation, she focuses her thoughts on food, specifically visualizing tuna and salmon.

When we are ready for self-change, we need tools to help us change. The more tools you have, the more solutions you have. There are many tools out there to help with self-improvement: e-learning (online video), onsite classroom training courses, and instructor-based meditation/mindfulness training. If you prefer to do it yourself, look for self-help or audio books that you can read or listen to at your leisure.

Remember to seek additional support systems when you need them (e.g., talking to family or a close friend, counseling, seeing your family doctor). When we begin using mindfulness and meditation as the tools for change, we first train to look at experiences nonjudgmentally and, therefore, learn to react less. Nonreactivity leads to unlearning of habitual thoughts and reactions, as the nonreactivity changes and creates new neuronal connections in the brain. The less we react, the stronger the neuronal connections get, and this helps in creating change in the brain and, ultimately, our behavior.

Reacting less is a tool to help you to ground yourself to return yourself to your natural self of peace and calmness (happiness). Many different types of meditations help with self-change. It all depends on what type of change you are looking for. The internet is an excellent source to find different types of meditations to help you with your needs. Here is an sample list of different types of meditations and their uses:

- *Concentrative practices (CP)*—sustaining attention (e.g., breathing, sounds, or bodily sensations)
- *Integrative body/mind therapy (IBMT)*—body relaxation, mental imagery, and mindfulness training
- *Mindfulness-based stress reduction (MBSR, developed by Dr. Jon Kabat-Zinn)*—calm the mind and body to help cope with illness, pain, and stress
- *Cognitively based compassion training (CBCT)*—compassion meditation practices
- *Insight meditation*—attention to internal and external sensory stimuli
- *Mindfulness*—awareness of what is happening in the present moment
- *Ecstatic meditation*—concentration on joy or happiness

If you find it difficult to relax or fall asleep, try using meditations that help you to relax—concentrative practices (CP), integrative body mind therapy (IBMT), or mindfulness-based stress reduction (**MBSR**). An example of this would be to focus your attention on your breathing, count your breaths, or do a body scan.

If you find it difficult to be positive, try using ecstatic meditations. For example, meditate on gratitude, and list all the things that you have in your life for which you are grateful.

If you find it difficult to let go of past resentments, or you are hard on yourself, try compassionate meditation—compassion/loving-kindness meditations).

If you find it difficult to focus on tasks and need to improve your concentration, try using concentrative practices (**CP**) that help you sustain attention on stimuli (e.g., sounds, breathing, bodily sensations).

Remember: It is not easy to work on yourself, but having an open mind to accept new ideas and knowledge and mastering new skills will create new neuronal connections within the brain, which expands new thinking. With time and practice, positive behavioral changes will occur.

Step 2: Stay in the Present—Connecting with Nature for Help

What is it about nature that helps us connect to spiritual wellness? A tree, a bird gliding through the sky, or a home garden can connect us to a state of peace. I have a friend who hikes in nature by himself for a week, and when he returns home, he describes his experience as *spiritual*. For him, this alone time walking through nature involves bringing about experiences toward peace and harmony.

My mother, who is retired, spends many hours attending to her garden. She finds it very therapeutic, as her mind is drawn away from problems to mindful activities in the garden. Nature can provide us with the environment to help slow down the mind. Again, we need mindfulness to allow us to see the beauty and wonders that nature has to offer. A quiet moment spent on a meandering path creates opportunities to practice mindfulness. Being one with nature is to have the mind immersed in the present moment. I often find that a twenty-minute walk in nature boosts my spirit.

A nature experience does not have to be restricted to the bush or forest; it also can include a walk in the park. If walking or gardening is not your thing, then might I suggest growing a plant, inside or outside your home, to connect with nature. The simple joy of taking care of a plant connects us with the beauty of life because. Stop and think for a moment—this plant only needs water and light from us; otherwise, it grows on its own. If you need to be more involved with your plant, how about growing a bonsai tree? Bonsai trees provide opportunities to grow and develop them. The activity of shaping a bonsai to mimic the shape of a full-size tree takes training and practice. It is through the process of skillfully developing the bonsai that one finds mindfulness and the connection to nature. As thoughts become focused, a state of peace and balance can be reached.

Many times, I have walked the paths along rivers and have witnessed deer. One time, I was walking along a river on a cold day in December. For a short time, it snowed heavily. I was near the riverbank and was sheltered from the falling snow by the trees. At that very moment, I looked across the river and saw a family of deer far on the other side—three deer in total. I imagined it was a mother and two of her fawns. There was very little wind, but in that moment, I felt the air. I felt the stillness of the water and trees and the silent movement of the deer. My mind was so immersed in that experience that I felt a profound sense of joy. My mind was clear, and there was no judgment or analysis of any kind for that moment, just a feeling of wonder. The beauty of that scene reached deep within my inner being and radiated a wonderous feeling of respect for nature and its wonders. When I returned home that day, I felt as if my spirit was renewed.

Many of us can share similar stories of a nature moment, when we experienced being totally present in the moment (whether we knew it or not). And when asked to tell the story, we are able to give vivid details of what transpired, but we might say, "Words cannot explain." When we feel something profound, we find ourselves looking again and wanting to experience those same moments.

I do find myself grasping or wanting to experience again the snow/river/deer experience, but then, at that moment, I realize that this is grasping the past. I remind myself to stay in the present moment. As I continue to take walks in nature, I try to focus my awareness in the surroundings. When my mind starts to wander, I try to shift focus on to different sights or sounds. Nature—just like prayer, meditation, or alone time—can aid us to become fully present. The key is to keep trying to stay in present awareness.

Step 3: Everyday Life

In between meditation, prayer, reflective time, and alone time is the rest of life. We have families to take care of, school and jobs to attend, meals to prepare, and household chores to complete. Then there are the in-between things—showering/bathing, grooming, dressing, eating, drinking, paying the bills, driving, and leisure (and the list goes on). How do we bring greater awareness to ourselves and, at the same time, continue to self-improve?

My personal experience has been that both awareness and self improvement are continuous and never-ending. Because our minds are not perfect, there is always something to improve on. To become a pianist, you need to practice every day. Similarly, to transcend thoughts, emotions, fears, worries, and doubts, we need to use our tools every day. Daily practice in mindfulness and meditation helps to deal with unmindful thoughts and actions. And in time, daily practice becomes habitual practice, which then creates new neuronal connections in the brain, thus allowing change to occur. With new thought processes, the mind becomes quieter and calmer, allowing a better insight into your true self. The journey begins with accepting new ideas, knowledge, and skills and then putting them into practice. Training the mind is like training the puppy, with never-ending patience and kindness.

In everyday life, there are so many opportunities to practice. As you wake in the morning, take five minutes of mindful breathing before getting out of bed. This is a good time to help bring a steady calmness to the mind before it becomes active with thoughts. Try to enjoy something special about the morning: a flower that bloomed, the sound of birds, or the wind in the trees. Pick one activity per day in which you will commit to mindful practice. For example, while brushing your teeth, try to focus on the task. If your mind starts to wander, bring it back on the task.

As you improve, pick more mindful activities (eating, drinking, paying your bills, etc.). While you are driving or while stopped at a red light, take some deep breaths, and pay attention to your breathing. When you arrive at your destination, take a few moments to breathe, consciously and calmly, relaxing your body. If you are at work or at school, while sitting at your desk or computer, become aware of any tension. Once you become aware of any signs of stress or physical tension, take a break to stretch or walk.

Before you enter your home, consciously take a few calming and relaxing breaths. As you go to sleep, practice some *letting go* meditation by taking slow, mindful breaths. Look for any opportunities throughout the day to practice meditation and mindfulness. And remember to be patient and kind with yourself, as your mind has been conditioned to think and act a certain way. It takes time for the mind to get used to this type of practice.

CHAPTER SEVEN

Happiness Teachings

IN MY PURSUIT TO UNDERSTAND HAPPINESS AND SUFFERING, I have come across many great sources of information—books, spiritual teachers, and online teachings and videos. Many great people are willing to offer advice and help, as they—like you and me—are looking for the same thing in life, and that is to be happy.

There are, however, two particular sources of information that I would like to share with you. The first source comes from the teachings of Jesus Christ, and the second comes from the Buddha. These teachings together provide great insight into happiness and suffering from the perspective of both theory and practice. In terms of theory, we get an insight into the causes of suffering. Regarding practice, the teachings provide spiritual pathways to help unveil happiness within ourselves.

These teachings and their pathways are for everyone, regardless of age and independent of any religious background. Once we put away our fears and open our minds to new ideas and knowledge, we can learn to master new skills that will positively enhance our well-being.

Both Jesus and the Buddha taught that happiness requires spiritual practice. Why spiritual practice? Recall that spiritual practice involves both actions and activities to bring about experiences and development toward peace and inner calm. When we participate or take action in the form of spiritual practice, we engage in our development of happiness. Some spiritual practice involves spending time alone in meditation, prayer, or other alone time. This type of practice helps us to develop mindfulness, as we become more aware of our thoughts and feelings. In addition, both meditation and prayer connect to our true inner selves and spiritual natures. These spiritual practices also develop concentration, which helps remove both physical and mental distractions, bringing us closer to a total peace of mind. The Buddha taught that with a total peace of mind, a sense of bliss is achieved.

Then there is the spiritual practice that involves the service to others. Helping others is the key to happiness. Happiness comes from the transformation of the inner self to recognize that giving. without expectations or expecting something in return, leads to a profound inner joy. By helping others, you feel good about yourself.

As social beings, we all need each other, and we all inherently feel happy when we are involved in service to others.

Sometimes it can be difficult to deal with people, but the more awareness you can apply to your thoughts, the better you will respond to yourself and to others. As the saying goes, no man is an island. We all need each other. And remember service to others also means that sometimes we need to receive service too.

Let's look at teachings of Jesus Christ and the Buddha.

Jesus Christ—The Sermon on the Mount

There is a teaching called the Sermon on the Mount from the Gospel of Matthew. In the Sermon on the Mount, Jesus Christ gives a talk while on a mountain, describing how to find happiness. Jesus describes several wonderful pathways that respond to the inner desire for happiness. These teachings are called the Beatitudes, and there are eight of them. The eight Beatitudes show us the meaning of happiness and how to achieve it. The following are the eight Beatitudes (Matthew 5:3–12 NIV):

1. Blessed are the poor in spirit, for theirs is the kingdom of heaven.
2. Blessed are those who mourn, for they shall be comforted.
3. Blessed are the meek, for they shall inherit the earth.
4. Blessed are those who hunger and thirst for righteousness, for they shall be satisfied.
5. Blessed are the merciful, for they shall obtain mercy.

6. Blessed are the pure in heart, for they shall see God.
7. Blessed are the peacemakers, for they shall be called children of God.
8. Blessed are those who are persecuted for righteousness' sake, for theirs is the kingdom of heaven.

Let us explore each Beatitude in some detail to understand its meaning.

1. Blessed are the poor in spirit, for theirs is the kingdom of heaven.

In this first Beatitude, Jesus gives direction on happiness or well-being. *Poor in spirit* recognizes that happiness lies inside us and not in the outside world. The word *poor* refers to a lack of attachment. We attach ourselves or hold on to many things. Let's start with the most obvious. We hold on to material things. *Defining who you are by external things can change your happiness.* Material things can change; therefore, your happiness can change. Our minds are never satisfied, even as we get what we want (e.g., new car, new house, new furniture). The mind might be happy for a short time, but then it looks for other things it wants to get. This thirst will never be quenched. Remember that happiness resides in the inner dimension of our well-being, not in the outer (physical or material things).

To what other things do we attach ourselves? Next is the ego. Recall the meaning of ego identification—when we define who we are through the stage of life we are in, our occupations, or a mental position. The more we can lose our egos, the greater the happiness. In this Beatitude, when we can detach ourselves from physical/material things and let go of our egos, we gain happiness. When we can see ourselves as spiritual beings, we open ourselves to God to help us increase our level of awareness to our beings so that self-change can occur. The closer we get to our true beings, the greater the power in sustaining happiness and avoiding suffering. Happy are those who can let go of material attachment and ego identification.

2. *Blessed are those who mourn, for they shall be comforted.*

When we mourn for someone, we display outward expressions of our sadness. For example, at funerals, wearing black is an outward sign of mourning. Sadness is our emotional state, while mourning is our physical expression. If we can accept our sadness (anxiety, anger) and work with our feelings in a mindful way (meditation), then we can let go of the attachment of this emotion. When bad things happen, we can learn not to react but to respond with nonjudgment and to accept these things, which allows us to let go. The process of letting go allows us to avoid suffering. The process of mourning is saying our final goodbyes when we have lost someone. Similarly, the process of mourning is letting go of all the things that we hold on to that keep us suffering, such as clinging onto our thoughts, emotions, and resentments. Happy is the person who can let go to thoughts, emotions, and resentments when bad things happen.

3. Blessed are the meek, for they shall inherit the earth.

In this Beatitude, Jesus's definition for *meek* can be gentle, humble, or egoless. Big ego equals big suffering. Happy is the person who can learn to let go of his or her ego, or the need to be right, or the need to defend a mental position. Recall the story of the two friends who were walking down their street, and one friend noticed that a neighbor had purchased a brand-new expensive car. This story implies that when we can drop our egos, we can appreciate and share in the good fortune of others. Suffering comes when our egos start judging or comparing our inadequacies to someone's good fortune. Happy is the person who can respond instead of react to his or her ego.

4. Blessed are those who hunger and thirst for righteousness, for they shall be satisfied.

We are all spiritual beings. We all want to be happy, and we all want to avoid suffering. When we are connected with our inner dimension (spirit/soul), we not only wish ourselves to be happy and avoid suffering, but we also wish it upon others. When we hunger and thirst for righteousness, we have a strong desire for ourselves and others to be in balance with our thoughts, emotions, and actions. We want to be right with ourselves by connecting to our true inner selves. We want to be right with others by having mindful thoughts and mindful actions. We want right (mindful) thoughts and actions for the rest of the world so that others can connect to their true beings. Happy are those who are fully aware of their true natures and are connected with their true spiritual selves.

5. Blessed are the merciful, for they shall obtain mercy.

Let go of blame, resentment, anger, and hatred. Let go of the story. Let go of the *coconut*. Let go of the ego. Respond rather than reacting. You have the choice to walk away. Practice cultivating loving-kindness and compassion meditation. Forgive yourself and forgive others. Be kind to yourself and be kind to others. Stay in the present moment. "Forgiveness is not about releasing them, it's about releasing yourself from the pain of anger and resentment and transforming it into empathy and understanding".[8] Happy are those who can let go and show loving-kindness and compassion to themselves and others.

6. Blessed are the pure in heart, for they shall see God.

"Love and do what you will" (Saint Augustine). Connect to a state of happiness and peace by moving your mind to your true inner self, devoid of ego, resistance, and grasping. Wish yourself and others to be happy and avoid suffering. Seek gratitude, appreciation, optimism, and other desirable attributes. Desire to think and do good. Happy are those who continually reflect, pray, and seek ways to improve or learn to become a better

---

[8] Timothy Barlow, "It's All Good: Forgiveness comes easier if you forgive yourself first," Vaughan Citizen, April 23, 2014, 1.

person inside. In learning how to be a better person, you will help avoid unnecessary suffering for you and others.

7. Blessed are the peacemakers, for they shall be called children of God.

Our reactions can produce suffering for us or others. Learning to respond rather than reacting can lead to a more peaceful solution and the road to happiness. The road to peace starts with responding to yourself by forgiving and being kind to yourself instead of self-criticism (reacting). In chapter 1 (see step 4 of "How to Let Go of Your Ego"), we discussed that we have a choice to respond rather than reacting. If someone says something hurtful, you can choose to acknowledge the person's comment, excuse yourself, and walk away. If you decide to stay, try putting an end to the comment and move on to the next topic. If you need to respond, rather than a defensive or offensive comment, try a loving-compassionate comment, such as, "I think you are a better person than that."

When something goes wrong, our minds look for blame because our minds do not know how to deal with our negative emotions (e.g., anger, frustration, judgement, hatred). We may blame the world, society, or God when bad things happen.

No amount of blame will change anything that has already occurred. Instead, the blame will only lead to the situation getting worse and will cause greater suffering to you and others.

We may continue to blame God because we think that God, who created this problem, can also reverse it (via a miracle, or cure). Blaming God for the problem and then praying to God for a solution is contradictory. Praying is a spiritual practice involves both actions and activities to bring about experiences and development toward peace, harmony, and finding purpose in life. Blaming is our mind's reaction to irritation. Praying and blaming are opposites. We first must deal with our negative emotions by taking positive steps to deal with the irritation (i.e., meditation). We can pray to ask for strength to help us deal with the negative emotions. As we accept the irritation, we respond with kindness and compassion toward ourselves. Happy are those who can respond and deal with their irritation to bring about peace and harmony.

8. *Blessed are those who are persecuted for righteousness' sake, for theirs is the kingdom of heaven.*

If you can learn to extend happiness (peace) beyond meditation and into day-to-day activities, then no matter what happens, you will be in a state of equanimity. Your mind will be balanced or undisturbed by thoughts, emotions, and pain. This is called being enlightened. It can be very difficult to deal with people, but the more awareness you can apply to your thoughts, the better you will respond to yourself and others. When others are unmindful, their thoughts, speech, and actions can disrupt their happiness and cause suffering to themselves and others. To become a pianist, you need to practice every day. Similarly, spiritual practice betters us by helping us to transcend suffering. Daily practice in mindfulness and meditation and prayer help us deal with others' unmindful thoughts and actions. Happy are those who stay mindful amid unmindful thoughts, speech, and actions.

The Eight Beatitudes—Summary

Jesus Christ teaches us to desire to think and do good; to wish ourselves and others to be happy and avoid suffering; to stay mindful amid unmindful thoughts, speech, and actions and respond with loving-kindness and compassion to bring about peace and harmony; to seek gratitude, appreciation, optimism, and other desirable attributes; to continually reflect, pray, and seek ways to improve or learn to become a better person inside and to become fully aware of our true selves and spiritual natures; to let go of ego, resentment, grasping, resistance, and material attachments. Jesus said, "Love each other as I have loved you" (John 15:12 NIV). This type of love is free from conditions, history, indiscretions, prejudice, race, or background. If there is love in whatever you do, happiness is there beside it.

The Buddha—The Four Noble Truths and the Noble Eightfold Path

Gautama Buddha, commonly known as the Buddha, taught about gaining insight to suffering and how to transcend it. The Buddha's teachings, called the Four Noble Truths, can be summarized as follows:

- The First Noble Truth: there is suffering (*dukkha*) in this world. For example, there is sickness, aging, death, stress, pain, and sorrow.
- The Second Noble Truth: the origin of suffering comes from mental afflictions (e.g., grasping, craving, resisting, attachment, ignorance).
- The Third Noble Truth: there is a way out of suffering by freeing the mind from attachment. Sickness, aging, and death cannot be avoided, but fear and worry regarding them can be passed over (i.e., through detachment or letting go).
- The Fourth Noble Truth: the path to overcome suffering is through wisdom, morality, and meditation (concentration).

The Four Noble Truths explain that suffering (dukka) is inevitable. Suffering arises from sickness, aging, death, and pain. Suffering also comes from our mental afflictions. We can stop suffering if we learn to respond instead of reacting to our thoughts and emotions. The Buddha taught that if we want to overcome suffering (and even transcend it), we need to follow and practice the Noble Eightfold Path. This path is divided into three parts: (1) insight (wisdom), (2) morality (conduct), and (3) meditation (concentration). The Eightfold Path uses knowledge, in the form of gaining wisdom, and combines it with a spiritual life (i.e., morality) and spiritual practice (i.e., meditation and mindfulness) to reach freedom from suffering and to obtain ultimate peace (happiness). Here is the Eightfold Path:

- **Insight (Wisdom)**
  1. Right view (right understanding)
  2. Right intent (having good intensions)

- **Morality (Conduct)**
  3. Right speech
  4. Right action
  5. Right Livelihood

- **Meditation (Concentration)**
  6. Right effort
  7. Right mindfulness
  8. Right concentration

Let us explore each path in detail to gain further understanding.

Insight (Wisdom)

1. *Right view* (right understanding) deals with understanding the reality of things and how they are connected to suffering. Having the right view helps us with having insight into cause and effect. Our actions have consequences (or karma), and having the wisdom to understand this helps us guide our behavior.
2. *Right intent* deals with having good intensions and selfless behavior that is away from our egos. Our intentions should be toward peace and not harming any person

or creature. Our thoughts impact our well-being. If we want to avoid suffering and be happy, our thoughts must be free from attachments (e.g., material things, ego), anger, hatred, and ill intent. Our thoughts and intent need to produce compassion, loving-kindness, and understanding for ourselves and others. We are all connected because we all wish to be happy and avoid suffering.

Morality (Conduct)

3. *Right speech* deals with saying nothing that hurts others, even yourself (self-criticism). Right speech is telling the truth and being polite versus being rude. Right speech is about not gossiping or trying to deceive others. Remember the famous saying: "If you have nothing nice to say, don't say anything at all." Far better to stop yourself from saying something hurtful than increasing your suffering by dealing with feelings of regret. Being silent to your thought reactions can give you the space to pause for a moment to see your thoughts more clearly and respond with right speech.
4. *Right action* deals with having peace and not exhibiting ill-intentioned behavior, with the intention of helping others to lead a more peaceful life. Our actions should not cause harm or injury, killing, or sexual wrongdoing (e.g., being unfaithful to our partners). Right action deals with moral and honorable conduct.

5. *Right livelihood* deals with our means of support, living, and income. Whatever profession or job you have must not bring harm to others. For example, your conduct in business should be virtuous. Not harming others means you do not engage in cheating, lying, scheming, spying, backstabbing, or any other unethical behavior.

Meditation (Concentration)

6. *Right effort* deals with putting effort into moving our thoughts and emotions from reacting to responding to generating higher levels of loving-kindness and compassionate thoughts. The lowest level of thoughts and emotions are those that react. It is here where our minds inherently react to produce suffering. At this level, we have worry, fear, irritation, anger, resentment, and hatred. These thoughts and emotions can be toward ourselves, someone else, or things. With the right effort, we can move up to the next level of responding thoughts and emotions. At this level, we deal with our thoughts and emotions through various ways to help us accept, detach nonjudgmentally, and, finally, let go of them. The next level of right effort is making or creating good thoughts and emotions. At this level, we engage in loving-kindness, compassionate, and joyful thoughts and emotions. Ultimately, we strive for a state of equanimity (or nirvana).

7. *Right mindfulness* deals with becoming aware of our thoughts, feelings, and actions in the present moment. Right mindfulness enables us to notice our thoughts and emotions in a nonjudgmental way, so as to be at peace with whatever is. When the mind is without self-awareness, unmindful thoughts can lead to hurtful words and actions that create suffering for ourselves and others.
8. *Right concentration* deals with using concentrative practices to train the mind to help sustain attention. Right concentration deals with meditation. The path of meditation has many stages that one goes through to finally reach total happiness and peace of the mind.

According to Buddha, there are four stages of deeper concentration called Dhyana:

- The first stage of concentration is one in which mental hindrances and impure intentions disappear and a sense of bliss is achieved.
- In the second stage, activities of the mind come to an end and only bliss remains.
- In the third stage, bliss itself begins to disappear.
- In the final stage, all sensations including bliss disappear and are replaced by a total peace of mind, which Buddha described as a deeper sense of happiness. [9]

---

[9] The Pursuit of Happiness Organization, https://www.pursuit-of-happiness.org/history-of-happiness/buddha, accessed 11/8/21.

Summary: The Four Noble Truths and the Noble Eightfold Path

The Buddha taught that there is suffering in this world. Some suffering is inevitable (e.g., pain, sickness, aging), and some comes out of our own minds (mental afflictions). The Buddha also taught that there is a way out of suffering. He explained that it takes knowledge and spiritual practice. When we learn and gain wisdom, we can understand suffering and happiness. For example, we understand that all our actions have consequences (or karma); as such, for every action there is a reaction. Learning to be mindful of our thoughts and actions can help us move away from reacting, giving way to responding.

What we say and do today will inevitably decide our fate in the future; hence, we need spiritual practice to help guide our speech and actions. This practice is in the form of right service to others and right concentration. Right service to others is having the right thoughts, intentions, and conduct toward others. Right thoughts and intent need to produce compassion, loving-kindness, and understanding for ourselves and others, with the desire for happiness and avoiding suffering. Right conduct involves saying and doing nothing to hurt others. Even our livelihoods must not bring harm to others.

In terms of right concentration, the Buddha taught that the practice of mindfulness and meditation is necessary to move our thoughts from reacting to responding. With greater effort (or practice), we can move our thoughts to joy and finally to a state of equanimity. Through mindfulness, we notice our thoughts and emotions in a nonjudgmental way, and we are at peace with whatever is. Through deeper meditation, we can train our minds to reach total happiness.

CHAPTER EIGHT

Pain and Suffering—
The Teacher of Happiness

IT WAS VERY DIFFICULT FOR ME TO WRITE THIS CHAPTER, INCLUDing its title. The difficulty came in trying to explain how experiencing pain and suffering could possibly lead to happiness. Just thinking about pain creates suffering in our minds. Seeing our loved ones suffer in pain can create suffering for ourselves as well. No parents wish their children to experience pain. As parents, we do everything possible to protect our children from experiencing any pain. I have heard that sometimes it's not good to shelter our children from suffering, but the argument here is that *that's not life*. As the Buddha said, pain and suffering are inevitable. Preparing our children for some suffering and pain is good for them.

As for me, I do everything possible to avoid pain, and I

also do everything possible to help my family avoid pain and suffering. Try not to look at my view as either right or wrong but simply a desire to want and my family and me to be happy and to avoid suffering. In my heart, I know there will be situations in which I cannot stop or protect family members from pain (e.g., sickness).

I also try to protect Abby from pain. Abby is now seventeen years old, which is eighty-four in human years. She has arthritis in her back leg, and I know she is somewhat in pain as she limps and is no longer able to jump onto the couch. When we or others experience pain, no one ever says, "This suffering is good for me." There are, however, some exceptions; for example, in martial arts, people train to develop a high tolerance to pain. Even in performance training, the saying is, "No pain, no gain"—the understanding being that if you want to build strength and stamina, your body needs to experience a level of discomfort. I guess there are some examples where pain is subjectively good. But in this chapter, the pain that I am referring to is the physical pain that comes from things like disease, aging, trauma, and other medical conditions that create pain, rather than emotional pain, which I call suffering.

What is the relationship between pain and suffering? Say, for example, you're preparing a meal, and you accidentally cut your finger on a knife. Let's assume that the cut is small enough that you don't even need a Band-Aid. At first, there might be an initial sensation or physical discomfort, which we call pain. Since the cut is so small, there is not much thought about what happened.

Let's say, however, that the accident resulted in a large cut to your finger, large enough that it requires at least two Band-Aids to stop the bleeding. This type of cut results in a greater sensation of pain. Because you need at least two Band-Aids, there might be initial worry about the injury. This worry comes from the mind, and that is called suffering. Your mind inherently and automatically reacts to the accident and creates thoughts and feelings of worry.

Now let's say that the cut to the finger is so deep that it requires stitches and possibly painkillers. The level of pain has increased and, most likely, so has our suffering. In addition to worry, the mind now creates fear of what might happen with the injury to your finger. You might worry about different scenarios: *How long will it take for the finger to heal? How will I be able to do daily chores if I can't move my finger? How will I do my job?* And so on. In addition, you might become angry or feel frustrated because of the inconveniences that will result from this accident. Your mind might look for blame as to the causes of this accident. You might fault the dull knife. You might blame the kids for causing you to not pay attention to what you were doing. You might criticize yourself for being "stupid."

Again, the mind can create all this suffering from a single cut to the finger. In these three examples, we see several observations regarding the relationship between pain and suffering. The first is that pain is defined as a physical sensation that results in discomfort, while suffering comes from our mind. The second relationship is that the greater the pain, the greater the suffering—but this is not always true. My grandfather was a beekeeper and would get repeatedly stung when he was working with his bees. For him, the discomfort he felt did not result in any suffering because both his mind and body were accustomed to the bee stings. But for someone who has an allergic reaction to bee stings, this could be a life-threatening situation. The relationship between pain and suffering can change, but I think it's fair to say that pain can lead to suffering.

The Buddha said that the origin of suffering comes from mental afflictions. What does this mean regarding pain? When Abby is limping because of her arthritis, the discomfort or pain that she is feeling is there. The wonderful thing about cats is that they do not suffer from mental afflictions. Abby does not worry about her arthritis in terms of future problems, nor does she grasp how things were when she was young and free from the arthritis. Abby thinks and lives only in the present moment.

Mental afflictions come from thinking about the past and worrying about the future. If you ever have had a sore back, you get with it both pain and suffering. The pain comes from the physical discomfort whenever you try to move your back; the suffering comes from the emotional turmoil you go through. The pain can be managed with medication, but you are still left with unwanted thoughts and emotions. You worry about how you will be affected in managing your tasks or your job. You imagine scenarios and analyze them to death. With your thoughts on the future, you create unnecessary suffering.

Something interesting, however, happens if you can catch your mind when it does occur. There are times when the mind is forced to be in the present moment, which usually occurs when pain sets in. You could be ruminating about something, and suddenly, you feel a sharp pain, which then causes your mind to move from ruminating thoughts to the present moment. With your mind focused on the pain, you cautiously move and notice every movement that you make in an attempt to prevent further pain and injury. During this time, your mind is focused and absent from worry and fear. In this mindful awareness, your thoughts are on your actions, as you cautiously move about, to ensure that what you do will limit additional pain. With each step, twist, and bend, your mind is completely in the present moment; you are fully aware of every thought and action that occurs. In this exact moment, your mind is free from mental afflictions.

I would like to share a personal story: One Sunday, my wife, daughter, and I were coming home from my father-in-law's cottage. Over the weekend, I had started to have heart palpitations. At the time, I was not sure what it was because I felt this discomfort in my stomach area. My family has a history of acid reflux—my mother has it, and my grandfather had it all his life. And, of course, I have it. I attributed these new sensations to my stomach issue.

When we arrived home that evening, the heart palpitations continued, to the point where it was difficult to fall asleep. The next day, the heart palpitations began after breakfast and continued throughout the entire day. That evening, I decided to go to the local hospital, as I was not sure if this was a stomach issue or something to do with my heart.

When I arrived at the emergency department, they checked

my blood pressure, took some blood, monitored my heart, and took a chest x-ray. The doctor said I showed signs of heart palpitations, but there was no indication of any serious heart issues. He said that everything seemed fine, but he recommended that I see a cardiologist and also get an endoscopy to check the inside of my stomach.

The next day, I called to make an endoscopy appointment. I was lucky because they had an appointment available the following day. I had an appointment the following week at the heart diagnostic clinic. The night before the endoscopy appointment, the nurse told me not to drink or eat anything after midnight. That evening when I went to bed, besides having the heart palpitations, my stomach felt irritated. In the middle of the night, I woke up and had anxiety—I feared I wouldn't be able to fall asleep, and I feared I wouldn't be able to calm my stomach without something warm to drink, like an herbal tea. As I was lying in bed, the anxiety led to a panic attack, and I felt hot and flushed with sweat. My mind felt out of control as my thoughts raced.

At that moment, I asked myself, *Do you want to continue to suffer?* I answered, *No, I do not want to suffer.* My mind responded, *Then you need to focus on the present moment, and you need to accept what is happening to you at very moment without fear and worry.* I had to *accept*, without resisting, how I was feeling. I began breathing slowly and focused on my breath. My thoughts kept streaming, but I simply accepted them and tried not to judge any of them.

In my body, my stomach was irritated, and the heart palpitations continued. I simply opened myself up to accept the physical sensations that were occurring at that moment. I recognized and accepted that I had anxiety, and I focused on the breathing and visualized breathing *into* the physical sensations. I asked myself, *What do I need in this very moment?* And I responded, *I need to be held tight or get a big, long hug.* I visualized my wife holding me, and I visualized Jesus holding my hand, saying everything would be **OK**.

I said a prayer as if I already had received the strength to get through this. I continued to stay in the present moment, and I continued to allow what I was feeling and the thoughts that were generated without resistance. I felt at peace, and shortly afterward, I fell asleep.

I woke up the next morning around seven o'clock. The endoscopy appointment was not until 9:30. I again reiterated to myself that I didn't want to suffer and that I'd like to stay in the present moment and stay with any physical sensations. The palpitations and my upset stomach were still there, but I focused on these physical sensations and allowed any thoughts to pass without resistance. This was not an easy task, as my mind resisted staying in the present moment. I treated my mind, however, as if it was a puppy, and instead of getting upset by what the puppy was doing, I embraced my mind as a dear friend and said, *I will take care of you.*

I felt great relief and continued to focus on the present moment. When I arrived at the endoscopy clinic, the nurse took all the relevant information and escorted me to a room where preparations would begin. I felt my heart racing, as I began feeling nervous, but I was able to calm myself down; I told myself that I'd had this endoscopy procedure done in the past, and there was nothing to worry about. I again focused on my breath and on any sensations that I was experiencing.

I was finally brought into the room where the procedure would take place. The doctor explained what was going to happen and that the endoscopy procedure involved a general anesthesia. When I woke, I felt completely relaxed and calm, which had to do with the general anesthesia. The doctor saw me shortly after and reviewed his findings with me. The news was good; he said that there was no ulcer or cancer. He did note that, due to the acid reflux, I should continue to take medication to ensure that the stomach healed. I was relieved to hear the findings, and I shared the news with my wife as she drove me home.

When I arrived home, I still felt relaxed and calm. The doctor said that it would take several hours for the general anesthesia to wear off. He also said I should drink lots of fluids and relax. I took the doctor's advice and rested for the day. That evening, I went out for a walk with my wife, and I noticed my mind had started to think about the cardiologist appointment at the end of the week. Again, I said to myself, *Do I want to suffer, or do I want to be happy?* I answered, *I don't want to suffer.* Again, I made an effort to try to stay in the present moment.

After the walk, I continued with my daily meditation practice, which helped to reinforce the present moment. I also found it helpful to discuss with my wife how I felt and what I was going through. I continued to watch my thoughts and accept my emotions as best as I could. For the rest of that week (and through the weekend), I continued to stay focused in the present moment.

The following week, I went to the heart diagnostic clinic. They started the process with a heart ultrasound. Next, the technician fitted me with a heart monitor, called a *holter*. This device records the heart's rhythm. I was to wear this device for seventy-two hours and then return it and see the cardiologist the next day for results.

Trying to sleep that first night while wearing the device was somewhat uncomfortable, but eventually my mind and body got used to it. The next day, I became somewhat more aware of what I was doing and feeling. This awareness came out more from worry and not from mindfulness, as my mind didn't want to sabotage the recordings by doing anything crazy. With both mindfulness and meditation, I was able to calm down this thinking. At the end of the third day, I went back to the clinic, where they finally removed the holter.

The next day, my wife and I went to the clinic. I asked her to come in with me to hear the results. The doctor said that the monitor did pick up some heart palpations, but it was nothing to worry about. The heart ultrasound confirmed that everything was working just right. We both felt relieved to hear the good news, but it left unanswered question: *why was I still having palpitations?* The doctor speculated on the reason but had no definitive answer.

Again, I caught my mind thinking and worrying about this. I asked my wife if we could try to solve the problem together or at least gain some clarity. We both came to the same conclusion—since the palpitations seemed to increase when my stomach was bothering me, there seemed to be a logical link. The final conclusion was this: *take care of the stomach and the palpitations will take care of themselves.*

In the next couple of weeks, I tested this theory by taking antacids throughout the day when the palpitations started; sure enough, it seemed to work. They did not disappear completely, but at least they were more manageable.

The physical suffering or discomfort that I experienced during this time resulted in a lot of mental suffering. I reached a point where I asked myself repeatedly, "Do I want to suffer?" And my answer always was, "No. Then stay in the present moment, and keep practicing your meditation." I made a conscious and continuous effort to stay in the present moment as much as possible. I kept reminding myself to be gentle with my *puppy mind*, as it had a hard time sitting still. Instead of criticizing or using harsh talk to myself, I tried to use kindness, compassion, understanding, and meditation to help bring back my puppy mind to the present moment.

It took this specific experience to wake me up further. My pain taught me that if I could stay in the present moment and use all the tools that I had learned, I could suffer less by:

- accepting thoughts and emotions nonjudgmentally;
- worrying less by not thinking about the future;
- analyzing less to reduce the storyline;
- grasping less on how things were once in the past;
- craving less for a specific outcome;

- praying and hoping more—not how I wanted the outcome to be but accepting how things unfolded nonjudgmentally; and
- showing myself kindness, compassion, and understanding.

Today, in this moment, I feel that I suffer less because of what I went through. Was my pain a teacher to happiness? Indirectly, *yes*, my pain was a teacher to happiness.

It takes something dramatic to wake us up. Pain and suffering can be very strong motivators to foster change and open our minds to new ideas and knowledge. And there is no shortage of pain and suffering. The variety of pain and suffering is endless in life. Each experience can vary in time and intensity. The death of a loved one can create a lifetime of endless openings of suffering. A cut to the skin brings brief physical discomfort and possibly initial fear or worry.

No one wants to suffer, but pain and suffering are part of life. We cannot remove pain from life, but we can remove suffering (or at least we can suffer less). With every step toward mindfulness, meditation, right insight, and right conduct, we move away from suffering and embark on happiness. We need to open our minds to accept change to happen. Why does it take something dramatic to open our minds? My experience tells me that people cannot change people.

You cannot change someone, even with the best interest at heart. Have you ever tried to convince a person to think or act differently? Have you ever tried to convince someone to stop smoking or drinking? If people not willing, they will not change or even open their minds. Having a life-altering experience still is no guarantee that someone will change. Change is never easy, as working on oneself takes a lot of courage and a lifelong commitment. This reason alone can discourage someone from wanting to change.

There are other reasons why people are unwilling or hesitant to change. For some, it might be because of fear. For others, it might be that they don't want to leave their comfort zones. What are your reasons for wanting to change or for not wanting or hesitating to change?

Now comes the big question: how does pain help us to be happy? Pain can motivate us to change, as we ultimately will remove or reduce suffering. Is there another connection between pain and happiness? Have you ever lost something that was precious to you and then later found it? The moment that you discovered your lost item, you felt an overwhelming sense of gratitude and joy. This sense of happiness makes you appreciate your item even more. You might take precautions to not lose it again.

Pain and suffering act the same way. When you are in pain or are suffering, you have *lost* your connection to happiness. Once the pain and suffering are gone (even for a moment), you again appreciate *finding* your connection to happiness again. This gratitude might not last long, but your mind still records the event. Each time this experience gets recorded, we essentially get a sense of more appreciation for the good days, and this appreciation could act as a motivator for change.

We must be careful, however, to be mindfully present to the appreciation. If we don't have an awareness of our thoughts and emotions, our mind can create grasping and nonacceptance. For example, we don't want to keep losing our connection to happiness; instead, we want to grasp to it. And we don't want to accept pain; instead, we want to push it away. This mental affliction to grasping and pushing away causes more suffering in the situation. To avoid this, we need to appreciate the relief when we are not suffering and not grasp happiness. If we try to grasp happiness, then the act of grasping creates unconscious thinking, which can lead to emotional suffering. Instead, we should focus on the feeling of appreciation, mindfully and nonjudgmentally, and simply view it as is.

Pain and suffering can be motivators to help us to change by helping us to appreciate the *good* days; they also can be motivators for our wanting to change. When the mind is ready to accept change, we are ready to seek a way out of unnecessary suffering to find the happiness that was always present but was lost within us. When we are ready to change, our outlook on life also changes. We see that good and bad days are no longer different; they are simply *as they are*. Situations are no longer judged as being good or bad but simply seen as neutral (recall the "maybe" story in chapter 3).

People are viewed alike, without judgment (and judgment is only in the form of judging the act, not the person). Pain and suffering are not looked at as being opposite from happiness but as simply part of life. When you have had enough of pain and suffering, ironically, the pain and suffering can motivate you to seek a different path and can help you to appreciate it. Pain and suffering are like a teacher who encourages you to open your mind and to learn new things. They do not, however, give you instructions; they help you to learn or understand something by the experience they give, and this can encourage you to accept the need for change.

Pain and Suffering—Empathy to Happiness

Abby normally sleeps in her bed throughout the day and night. In the evening, she likes to sit with us on the couch while we are watching TV. But this is not the only time that she likes to sit with us. Both cats and dogs can sense when you are ill. It is because they can identify the chemical scent from human illness. When I am sick (or someone else in the family is sick), Abby recognizes this, but she takes it a step further. If I'm lying down in bed or resting the couch due to flu, Abby wants to stay with me, with her body side by side, next to mine.

Sympathy is when Abby is sleeping in her own bed and feels bad that I have a cold, but *empathy* is when Abby climbs up in bed with me or on gets on the couch and is side by side with me, knowing how I feel because she has been through this before. Empathy connects our pain and suffering to someone because that someone has gone through the exact pain and/or suffering that we are going through. Pain and suffering open our hearts to bring out understanding, compassion, and love. We all share the feeling or the need to avoid suffering and pain.

Equally as important, we all are connected to empathy. When you have gone through an illness, disease, condition, or experience that led to suffering, you gain an understanding of what it means to suffer. This experience enables you to open your heart and share your understanding and compassion to another human being who is going through the same thing.

When my father was in his early eighties, he was diagnosed with Alzheimer's disease. Nothing could have prepared us for what would happen next. When describing Alzheimer's, you might say it is a disease that affects memory. Unfortunately, a person goes through several stages in Alzheimer's, including memory loss. If I could redefine Alzheimer's disease, I would call it, more accurately, a mental degenerative disease. As this disease progresses, so do the symptoms. It not only steals one's memory but slowly affects regions of the brain. The brain essentially does not know what to do. Alzheimer's patients do not know how to feed themselves, go to the washroom, walk, or even talk.

The disease also affects emotions, as it creates anxiety, for example, or obsessive behavior, mood swings, paranoia, anger, or violent behavior were there was none before. To make matters worse in my father's case, he was already confined to a wheelchair. In his early fifties, he developed cerebellar degeneration (the medical name is *idiopathic cerebellar atrophy*). This disease affected a region in his brain that controls fine muscle movement. My dad lost the ability to move his muscles in a controlled and fine manner. He had slow, unsteady, chaotic movements of his arms and legs and had slurred, slow speech. For example, if you want to touch your nose, you move your finger in a straight path to connect to it. But my dad was not able to move his hand in a straight path; instead, it moved more in a chaotic S motion. As such, he had difficulty walking, talking, and moving. As you can imagine, this experience was very tough for my dad and my family, especially for my mom, who took care of him. And then, twenty-seven years later, my father developed Alzheimer's.

In the last year before my dad passed away, he was in a long-term care home. Many of the people in this home had similar issues to my dad but varied in degree. I noticed that the struggles and suffering that the patients and their families experienced were the same as what my family and I were also going through. Each person wanted to be happy and avoid suffering. At the beginning, when I first arrived at the long-term care home, I did not see or feel any signs of happiness. I would ask myself how anyone could be happy there.

But the more time I spent there, the more I began to realize which roads led to happiness. I felt compassion for my dad, my mom, and the rest of my family. The compassion motivated me to do anything that I could to help my dad and my family. I also felt the need to help others around me at the long-term care home. I felt that even something as simple as listening to someone (the patients, their families, or the workers) would help.

When you see others suffer, you understand their frame of mind, and doing so can help you not to judge others or any situation. Compassion leads to understanding, and both lead to love. Love can be in the form of kindness and caring for others. At the long-term care home, there was no shortage of love. Random acts of kindness were everywhere, but I needed to look beyond the suffering. Where did I find happiness at this place? Each time I came to visit my dad, I came with the intention of understanding and bringing loving-kindness to him, my family, other patients, and the workers. And each time I left the long-term care home, I felt joyful and at peace. And this is happiness.

Pain and suffering open your heart through empathy, and this cultivates understanding, compassion, and love. My heart knew how others felt at the long-term care home because my family and I were going through similar experiences. I spoke to a friend from work whose dad was confined to a wheelchair because of Alzheimer's; he was also in a long-term care home. Again, our empathy for each other connected us as we shared similar stories of our dads and of our moms, who were affected the most because of taking care of our dads.

Similar struggles of both pain and suffering open your heart to see what another human being goes through and helps you to understand the suffering. As the Buddha taught, without right thoughts and right intent, you cannot produce understanding, compassion, and loving-kindness. And these feelings are necessary to help avoid suffering.

If there is love in whatever you do, happiness is there beside it.

Having a Bad Day? Receive Some Compassion, Comfort and Love Meditation

May the following meditation bring *you* much needed comfort and compassion for your suffering. May it bring you a kind reminder to be gentle with yourself and to develop a deep love toward yourself, and may it free you from any frustration or anger you may have.

Step 1: Take a couple of minutes to watch your thoughts to give your mind a pause from thinking. Simply watch your thoughts (and emotions, if they arise) without trying to add to or chase them. See them come and go. Notice them without judgment, accepting each thought (and each emotion) without any resistance. If you find yourself lost in thought or emotion, simply notice this, and return to watching them again.

Step 2: Visualize yourself surrounded by people (or a person), who in the past were very kind to you and touched your heart with their love. See yourself sitting in front of these people. See them gently putting their hands on your head and sending out compassion, comfort, and love toward you. If you have a hard time visualizing this, simply visualize comforting white light, filled with compassion and love, coming out of their hands and into your mind and body.

Step 3: Breathe this comforting light (filled with compassion and love) into you. Each time you breathe this in, try to feel this warm feeling reaching into an area in your mind or body where you need it the most. Let it soothe the troubled area.

Step 4: Keep breathing in this feeling of compassion and love, and guide it into the *next* area in your mind or body.

- If you start feeling agitated, frustrated, or angry, sense this as coming out of a place from fear or worry. Recognize the fear or worry—you can call it *fear* or *worry* to help gain some clarity and gain distance from it. Now, go back to being surrounded by the people who showed you love, and again feel their hands on your head, sending their compassion and love to you once again.

Step 5: Take several breaths, slowly in and out, and focus on the breath to gain concentration and peace. You are finished!

This type of meditation focuses on developing our healing power of love toward ourselves. We show unconditional compassion to ourselves to elicit feelings of wanting to be free from suffering and the causes of suffering. And we learn to accept any frustration or anger and to transform these strong emotions into empathy and understanding.

CHAPTER NINE

Are You Walking the Path of Happiness?

In this chapter, I will ask a total of twelve questions, with some review commentary to help you reflect with some direction. Let's begin!

1. Answer this question on a scale of 1 to 10, with 10 being very happy; 5 being average; and 1 being very unhappy: Day to day, how happy are you?
2. Answer this question on a scale of 1 to 10, with 10 being very calm and at peace; 5 being average, and 1 being very agitated or flustered: Day to day, what is your level or state of peace or calmness?
3. The definition of happiness is "being in a state of peace and knowing that, at this very moment, you

are complete and knowing you are a spiritual being." Using this definition of happiness, answer the following questions:
- Do you believe that you have the capability to be in a state of peace?
- Do you believe that you are complete?
- Do you believe that you are a spiritual being?

There are no right or wrong answers to the above. Whatever your answers are, they are what you believe them to be. The most important thing is to recognize how you feel regarding your happiness and your state of peace. Recognizing your answers can help you to be mindful of your thoughts and emotions.

You can use the above questions to help you gauge your level of happiness. If you find there is a difference in response to your level of happiness and your level of calmness, this could be a difference in perception. For example, on most days, I feel very calm, but I might not feel very happy. Why? This is because of my training in mindfulness and meditation. I use these tools to help me concentrate and feel more relaxed. Naturally, I feel more at peace than being happy. And the reason why I feel less happy is because my mind is looking for external things to bring me happiness. For example, I might be looking forward to eating a chocolate bar. I do recognize that the chocolate bar will give me some pleasure from the sugar, but I remind myself that my state of happiness is rooted not in the chocolate bar but inside of me. And this is useful information for me to know—that I still need to work on my perception of happiness.

This perception is telling me that I still rely on outside factors to make me happy. And this insight helps me to realize that when I rely on outside factors and when I don't get them, then my mind starts to blame things and people for why I am not happy.

The good news is that this mindful insight is helpful for me to recognize areas that need self-improvement. When it comes to mindfulness, I can use awareness to help me see when these thoughts of outside pleasure and blame become evident. Again, mindfulness can help me to see the thoughts as thoughts and accept them nonjudgmentally to let them go. This practice takes time and continuous effort.

In terms of meditation, I can use this practice to help me feel the emotions of blame to help deal with any irritation. In addition, meditation can also help me to reach states of tranquility, which, in essence, make me feel very happy.

It is important not to have an expected outcome when meditating; otherwise, you can get into the mental affliction of grasping. Simply accept what comes.

I hope that for question number 3, you were able to answer yes—that you believe you have the capability to be in a state of peace. This question means that we always have a choice to either respond or react to thoughts, emotions, or an experience. The greater awareness we practice, the greater capability we will have to respond and remain in a state of equanimity.

Everything that you need, including your capability to respond instead of reacting is already inside you because you are already complete. But like anything, to become better at it, you need to practice. If you answered *not sure* to the question, then just being aware of how you feel inside and being honest with yourself is the road to happiness. Certain situations will challenge our state of peace and happiness.

Maybe you are going through a difficult time right now. Maybe your suffering (and your pain) is making it difficult to feel at peace. At this moment, you could feel frustrated with life's situations, and you are not sure what to do. Maybe you just feel irritated or upset, and you are not sure why. Whatever the reason as to why you answered *not sure*, take comfort in knowing that our minds and bodies are not perfect, and this means that there is nothing wrong with you, and it's not your fault.

Every human being is broken in some way. Because of this, you cannot blame or be harsh with yourself. We were not equipped to handle every obstacle, problem, or situation and get a perfect outcome or result. Be gentle, kind, and compassionate toward yourself! If, because of your life's situation, you start to question yourself, know that you are a spiritual being, and there is no confusion in who you are. *I am a spiritual being, and I am connected to an inner source of peace.*

Because our minds and bodies are not perfect, we need to do the work to train ourselves to go beyond our thoughts and feelings to avoid unnecessary suffering and to gain emotional or mental peace. The means training in mindfulness, meditation, right wisdom (or insight), and right morality. Walking the path of happiness means daily mental training. What helps to motivate me is seeing some positive results in my life (specifically, positive changes to my behavior), which helps to reinforce the need to continue training.

Plus, a daily practice becomes a habit. As this habit becomes part of your life, you begin to see it not as a chore but as an encouraging moment in quiet time. If formal meditation is not possible for you, remember to take a few slow, deep breaths many times throughout the day, whenever you have a chance.

Mindfulness can be done anytime you choose. A mindful moment can be focusing on a specific activity. Any awareness of your thoughts and feelings brings mindful practice. Training in right wisdom (or insight) refers to expanding your knowledge of understanding the ways to inner peace and happiness. As a starting point, look for any books or any other sources of information on understanding the ways of meditation and mindfulness. Most of these sources will also touch upon right morality or personal development, guiding you (specifically, your thoughts and actions) on how to be happy and avoid suffering.

4. People today are more stressed than ever. Some key examples of why people are stressed are their jobs, health (including lack of sleep and unhealthy diet), money, family/relationships, and media distractions (e.g., phones, emails, internet). Please answer this question on a scale of 1 to 10, with 10 being no anxiety or stress; 5 being average; and 1 being a lot of anxiety or stress: Day to day, how anxious or stressed are you?

5. Please answer this question on a scale of 1 to 10, with 10 being "I don't dwell"; 5 being average; and 1 being

"I dwell a lot": How often do you dwell or ruminative on the same thought, feeling (e.g., fear, worry), or event (e.g., a grudge, offense, dislike)?

Questions 4 and 5 are interrelated because if you are stressed about something, someone, or a situation, the mind tends to dwell or ruminate on the same thought or subject, which creates mental suffering (stress) that persists and returns. Therefore, the greater the stress, the greater the dwelling on something; hence, a low score would be evident for both questions. If your stress level is low, but your mind still dwells on a specific thought, fear, or worry, this could be because the mind is great at storing and holding on to negative thoughts, emotions, and events. Our minds do this as an inherent property to protect us from the tiger hiding in the bush, back in cave-dwelling days. Today, the tiger is no longer there, but our minds still create untrue fear and worry through our thoughts and imagination.

Mindfulness equips us with self-awareness, which helps us to recognize and understand the signs of stress and habitual thoughts. This, in turn, helps us to respond (versus react) more effectively. When we can recognize the hidden tiger in the bush, we can find ways of skillfully working through our ruminating thoughts, fears, and worries. There are many skillful ways to work through this:

- Use compassion and kindness to deal with unpleasantry. Even when dealing with life's difficulties, the road to peace is through compassion and kindness. This means being friendly, gentle, and tender toward yourself, with the desire to be free from suffering and the causes of suffering. (See chapter 2 for "Tapping into and Creating an Abundance of Compassion and Kindness.")

- Use interoceptive awareness—the process of identifying our feelings in relation to the sensations generated within the body, to shift our focus to our emotions to help us slow down the mind and remove storytelling. A specific meditation tool that can help bring interoceptive awareness and help bring relaxation to areas of tension is called sensory awareness meditation (SAM). (See chapter 3 for more information.)

- In chapter 2, we introduced body scan meditation. This type of meditation helps you to recognize any stress or tension in your body. Learning to recognize the tension helps you to stop what you are doing, preventing any further harm, and then applying relaxation techniques to help you relax the tension.

- It is not the situation but your reaction that causes stress. Learning to watch your thoughts and emotions can help you to respond instead of react to a situation to help lower stress and ruminating thoughts. Remind yourself that you have both the tools and capability to let go (or "let go of the coconut"). And when all else fails, you have the choice to walk away.

6. Please answer this question on a scale of 1 to 10, with 10 being never; 5 being average; and 1 being quite often:

Do you make the opinions of others more important than your opinion of yourself?
7. Please answer this question on a scale of 1 to 10, with 10 being never; 5 being average; and 1 being quite often: How self-critical are you?

Questions 6 and 7 explore self-acceptance. We often find ourselves wishing to be someone else. We think that if we surround ourselves with the people we want to become that we will somehow change into them. But this does not happen; instead, it only results in suffering.

At this very moment, you and I are imperfect, and that is perfect enough for us to start accepting ourselves for who we really are. This does not mean that you should not try to improve who you are; it simply means you should accept and love who you are. You can work on accepting yourself in many ways. For example, you can use positive affirmations in the form of repeating kind words to yourself to help create good thoughts. Another tool is using counterconditioning meditation (see chapter 4) to help change your neuronal connections and create new thinking patterns and reinforce the brain to store positive thoughts. In addition, there is self-reflection, where you look inside yourself and write down all the positive and beautiful things about you. And remember that by learning to accept yourself and to nurture your strengths in the context of your environment, can you become a better you, like a rose in a garden.

Resistance

I read a story in a book by Pema Chödrön, a spiritual teacher, that I would like to share with you:

> One evening Milarepa returned to his cave after gathering firewood, only to find it filled with demons. They were cooking his food, reading his books, sleeping in his bed. They had taken over the joint ... Even though he had the sense that they were just a projection of his own mind—all the unwanted parts of himself—he didn't know how to get rid of them. So first he taught them the dharma (law and order). He sat on this seat that was higher than they were and said things to them about how we are all one. He talked about compassion ... Nothing happened. The demons were still there. Then he lost his patience and got angry and ran at them. They just laughed at him. Finally, he gave up and just sat down on the floor, saying, "I'm not going away and it looks like you're not either, so let's just live here together." At that point, all of them left except one. Milarepa said, "Oh, this one is particularly vicious." (We all know that one. Sometimes we have lots of them like that. Sometimes we feel that's all we've got.) He didn't know what to do, so he surrendered

himself even further. He walked over and put himself right into the mouth of the demon and said, "Just eat me up if you want to." Then that demon left too. "The moral of the story is, when the resistance is gone, so are the demons." [10]

I love this story and especially "when the resistance is gone, so are the demons." The last demon must have been very scary for Milarepa. To put himself into the mouth of the demon must have been very frightening. You can see that he almost had no choice but to surrender to his fear in an attempt to have peace in his life. By accepting his fear, he was able to accept himself and the situation and to work with his feelings, rather than denying or fighting them. Through this approach, he could move forward to allow change to occur naturally.

Take a moment and reflect upon the following two questions:

8. What are the top two things that you resist in life?

Think about any specific fear or worry that might be stopping you from moving forward. If not fear, it could be something about yourself that you have a hard time accepting. For example, maybe you have a hard time accepting criticism, or you are very sensitive to other people's remarks and take things personally. You might struggle with wanting to be different.

---

[10] Pema Chödrön, Start Where You Are: A Guide to Compassionate Living (Shambhala Publications, Inc., 1994), 47–48.

9. List a few ways that can help you to accept your demons from question 8. If you need some help, see if any of these work for you:

- ✓ Mindfulness
- ✓ Working with your emotions through meditation (e.g., feeling the fear, worry, or other emotions)
- ✓ Journaling
- ✓ Talking to family or a close friend
- ✓ Counseling

Letting go of our demons can be very difficult, as the mind has a natural tendency to hold on. To free the mind from this tendency to hold on means that we must accept the fear and then work with the emotion(s). This process is difficult because it is unpleasant to deal with strong emotions, such as fear or worry. This is where our resistance comes from, so it takes great courage to face and deal with unpleasantry. As Jesus said, "Blessed are those who mourn, for they will be comforted" (Matthew 5:4 NIV). If you can accept your sadness (anxiety, anger) and work with your feelings in a mindful way (meditation), then you can let go of the attachment to this emotion.

Spiritual Practice

When we participate or act in any form of spiritual practice (e.g., meditation, prayer, service to others), we engage in the development of our happiness.

10. Have you ever tried to be kind to someone (and with good intensions), but your help was misunderstood or unappreciated, or maybe you were accused of having an ulterior motive? A phrase that describes when acts of kindness backfire is, "No good deed goes unpunished." How do you motive yourself to be kind, and what are your reasons for wanting to help others?

Both Jesus and the Buddha taught that the desire to think and do good brings happiness. For example, giving without expectations, including not expecting something in return, leads to a profound inner joy because happiness is in what you do and is in the very act of giving. The consequences of what happens after your act of kindness are not important because they are out of your control. We cannot control how people act or what they say. If your help backfires, then notice it without judgment, and let it go. It does no good for you to worry about it. In fact, dwelling upon it creates suffering for you. Remember that you can deal with your worry through meditation by feeling the emotion (as previously discussed).

If one of your answers to question 10 was based on "I help you and you help me," then try to remember that if that an expectation is not fulfilled, it can lead to one's feelings being hurt for a variety of reasons: (1) feeling that the person does not care about you; (2) feeling that the person does not appreciate your time and effort; or (3) feeling that the expectation of "I help you and you help me" was not fulfilled. This is another reason why giving without expectations brings happiness.

In addition to helping others, other spiritual practices engage our response of wanting to be happy (and wanting to help others). *Prayer* is a spiritual practice, the path of which helps to bring peace and stillness. When we pray, we bring a greater awareness of ourselves and that of others. Prayer helps us to see and ask for help with the struggles that we encounter. We all are the same because our minds and bodies are not perfect; thus, we all share similar struggles. This commonality connects us to each other and helps to elicit compassion for ourselves and for others; it creates a desire to help.

Reflective time alone is another spiritual practice that helps in the development of happiness and builds resilience in helping others. Through reflection, we can see the areas of ourselves in which we want to improve. Spending time within yourself is important so that you can take care of yourself first. You might think this is selfish, but you are taking care of yourself so that you can be of service to help others. You can't give what you don't have. You are building your inner-strength muscles so that when the time comes, you can be ready to help. In addition, if you spread yourself thin, you will harm yourself and will not be able to help others properly.

Pain and Suffering

The stress of a disease, illness, or the death of a loved one can create strong thoughts, emotions, and feelings. Add physical pain to the situation, and you have a formula for amplifying thoughts and emotions. You can try to do everything possible to alleviate the physical discomfort, but alleviating mental anguish can be very difficult. The difficulty lies in managing your thoughts and emotions when you are suffering or in physical pain. During these times, strong feelings and emotions will arise, and thoughts become very scattered. In addition, it becomes very difficult to stay focused, and your judgment can become unclear.

11. Reflect on a time when you were in pain and/or were suffering. Ask yourself: how did I manage my thoughts, emotions, and feelings?

    If it helps, you can answer the question on a scale of 1 to 10, with 10 being "I managed my thoughts, emotions and feelings well"; 5 being average; and 1 being "I did not manage them well."

12. Answer this question on a scale of 1 to 10, with 10 being very calm (and mindful); 5 being average; and 1 being very agitated, nervous, or restless: How did you deal with the people around you?

As we struggle through our pain and suffering, we need to be gentle with ourselves. We need to show compassion and loving-kindness toward ourselves and not judge our thoughts, emotions, and feelings. You are not your thoughts, emotions, and feelings. They do not represent who you are! You are a spiritual being! Be gentle with yourself by taking as much time as you need to heal at your own pace, rather than whatever others expect. Seek additional support systems when you need them (e.g., talking to family or a close friend, counseling, seeing your family doctor). Try using meditation and mindfulness apps if you find it difficult to be mindful or to focus on your breath. The more tools you have, the more solutions you will have. The more you can heal yourself, the more you can help others. *Don't* downplay your struggle or add guilt by saying that others have it worse than you. You don't need that extra burden. Instead, know that you are not alone because somewhere out there, someone is going through the same pain or suffering that you are going through. Peace will find its way back into your mind, and over time, strong thoughts, emotions, and feelings will diminish.

When you are dealing with people, the more mindful you can become, the less you will react to your brain's automatic conditioned behavior. The more awareness you can apply to your thoughts, emotions, and feelings, the less likely your words and actions will cause more suffering to you and others. Remember the famous saying to help you become more mindful: "If you have nothing nice to say, don't say anything at all." Far better to stop yourself from saying or doing something hurtful than increasing your suffering by dealing with feelings of regret. Keeping your thought reactions silent can give you the space to pause for a moment and see your thoughts more clearly and then respond with right speech.

Remember these words: My mind resisted staying in the present moment, but I treated my mind as if it were a puppy. Instead of getting upset over what the puppy was doing, I embraced my mind as a dear friend and said, "I will take care of you."

CHAPTER TEN

Finding Goals and a Life Purpose

A YEAR AFTER MY FATHER-IN-LAW RETIRED, HE HAD A HEART attack. He had worked hard all his life; even when he was on vacation, he still worked. For him, the word *vacation* meant having extra time to build a deck, paint a room, or change the brakes on the car. When he retired, there was no longer a distinction between going to work and being on vacation. Retirement was now a permanent vacation for him to get things done. At first, he kept busy, but soon, he ran out of things to do. The to-do list became shorter as time passed. His life—and essentially, his self-identification—was in his working. Working was connected to his self-worth.

He had very few things to do, and his not knowing what to do with more time on his hands created stress, which, I believe, contributed to his heart attack. I have heard it many times from coworkers and friends who retired or were close to retiring—they felt a sense of fear or worry or panic in not knowing what to do next. Some of my friends who retired went back to work, either part-time or full time.

I don't want to paint the picture that this is the general rule because I have a middle brother who retired early in life, and he is enjoying his retirement. My middle brother does not simply occupy his time; instead, he has a purpose with goals, which makes him happy. For example, his purpose in life is to take care of his family. Both he and his wife volunteer their time to help at a food bank twice per week. In the summer, they belong to a softball league, playing on Sunday afternoons. He keeps my mom busy by taking her shopping, going to church with her, and enjoying a cup of coffee with her in the mornings. My brother also enjoys his time playing golf. He has goals and a life purpose.

How can we describe finding a purpose in life? *Finding a purpose in life* means to find something that drives or motivates your life. Since we all want to be happy, our prime motivator is to do things that make us happy and feel at peace.

We defined happiness: Happiness is being in a state of peace and knowing that, at this very moment, you are complete and are a spiritual being. We already understand that we can't look for or find happiness in the outer world (material things) because happiness is within us. We simply need to find ways to reach it. Finding a purpose in life means finding something that drives or motivates us to reach states of happiness, peace, and wholeness (or being complete). Recall this story:

In this bush a mother bird had built her nest. Yet in the mist of the angry sky, rushing waterfall, the mother bird sat on her nest in perfect peace. Why did the King pick this picture? 'Because' explained the King. 'Peace does not mean to be in a place where there is no noise, chaos or hard work. Peace means being in the midst of all those things and still being calm in your heart and mind.' [11]

The mother bird was in a state of peace not only because she was able to let go of the things around her but because she had a purpose in taking care of her nest. Through this experience, she was content. When we look for a purpose in life, we must start within ourselves, looking for experiences that allow us to be happy and at peace. Since happiness and peace are interchangeable, as both are interrelated and mean the same thing (according to our definition of happiness), we therefore have a glimpse of how we might find a purpose in life. The question to answer now is, how do we find our purpose in life?

Each person will have a different purpose in life. For some, it may to become rich and famous, travel the world, raise a family, take care of a loved one, help others, grow a business, become successful or have satisfying work, or fight for a cause. Abby's life purpose is very simple: sleep, eat (with the occasional

---

[11] Catherine Marshall, "Picture of Peace," in *Stories for the Heart*, ed. Alice Gray (Sisters, Oregon: Multnomah Publishers, 1996), https://frommyheart2u.wordpress.com/tag/catherine-marshall, accessed 11/8/21.

Finding Goals and a Life Purpose

handouts of tuna and salmon from the humans), and snuggle on the couch.

Each of the above purposes creates experiences that bring out the desire that we want to feel good. Say, for example, your purpose in life is to fight against poverty. You might be motivated to help the poor because it breaks your heart to see children starving. Seeing this injustice motivates your goals and actions. This might encourage you to coordinate a fundraiser. The experience of helping the poor by raising money leaves you feeling good about yourself and the fundraiser. Your life purpose of helping others has guided your thoughts, influenced your behavior, helped you to set goals, and even shaped your conduct.

But what happens if we are not mindful in our life purpose? I am going to stretch this next example to make a point. Say, for example, your life purpose is to dominate the world. Whatever your motivations are seem justifiable to you. You begin your conquest by dominating each country, which again makes you feel good. The consequences (e.g., death and destruction) of your domination are justifiable in your thinking. In this example, it is easy to see that your life purpose of dominating the world has brought dangerous suffering. Your thoughts, insights, behavior, and goals shaped your choice in your life's purpose.

Finding our purpose in life starts with being mindful of our thoughts, emotions, and feelings. The practice of mindfulness helps us to see and become more aware of our thoughts, thus allowing us to respond appropriately instead of reacting in an automatic or negative way. When we are able to see our thoughts, we can learn to become more aware of living our lives to the fullest by being and living in the present moment.

Mindfulness teaches us to notice our thoughts and emotions nonjudgmentally and to be at peace with whatever is. When the mind is without self-awareness, unmindful thoughts can lead to hurtful words and actions that create suffering for ourselves and others. With mindful awareness and reflection, we can ask ourselves if we are reacting or responding to a thought, emotion, or experience.

Here are some examples of reacting versus responding:

1. Sue did not get the promotion for which she applied. She reacted to this experience by telling herself that she would never get a promotion.
2. Mary was feeling very lonely. She decided to go to a party, but she didn't meet anyone. She reacted by telling herself that nobody liked her, people were cruel, and she did not want to have new friends.
3. Bob received a letter from the university, rejecting his application to the master's program. He accepted this news with equanimity and responded by deciding that he would take some additional courses to help raise his marks, and then he would apply again next year.

Both Sue's and Mary's reactions resulted in negative thinking and stopped them from reaching their goals to connect to their life's purposes. Bob, on the other hand, decided not to let his disappointment, frustration, and anger take control of his thoughts. With calmness, he took time to reflect and decided to continue to pursue that which he loved.

By being mindful to our thoughts, we learn to respond and not react. And when we respond, our thoughts and intentions need to produce compassion, loving-kindness, and understanding for ourselves and for others. By responding appropriately, we can remove the barriers that prevent us from reaching our peace and happiness.

In example 1, when Sue did not get a promotion, she became disappointed, frustrated, and angry. Sue thought that she could never again get a promotion. Feelings of disappointment, frustration, and anger are all normal, but Sue could work to remove those barriers by responding with compassion, loving-kindness, and understanding for herself. When her thoughts and intentions have compassion, loving-kindness, and understanding, she can work and remove disappointment, frustration, and anger, which are barriers to her peace and happiness.

When we have compassion and loving-kindness toward ourselves, we can get through these moments and understand our pain and where it is coming from. From this point of healing, Sue would once again know that it is possible to get a promotion.

In example 2, Mary's disappointment in not meeting anyone at the party resulted in her harsh reaction toward herself and others. Responding with self-compassion and loving-kindness would help to prevent self-blame and self-hatred.

The need for our thoughts and intentions to produce compassion, loving-kindness, and understanding for ourselves and for others helps to remove barriers. When our intentions are free from attachments, frustration, disappointment, doubt, worry, blame, resentment, bitterness, anger, revenge, hatred, jealousy, guilt, and fear, we remove all these barriers to happiness. These same barriers prevent us from finding our purpose in life.

In example 3, Bob acknowledged his feelings and worked through them with calmness and reflection. His tools for calmness and reflection were meditation and mindfulness. He allowed kindness and compassion to enter his heart, allowing him to go beyond blame and hatred. By positioning himself to want peace, he was able to avoid suffering and reach the happiness that was already inside him. Bob's goal of getting into the master's program was not his life's purpose. Bob's purpose in life was to be happy, regardless of the circumstances or life's situations. It is the journey, not the outcome, that matters.

If we want to avoid suffering and be happy, our thoughts need to be free from attachments (e.g., material things, ego), anger, hatred, and ill intent. Our thoughts and intent need to produce compassion, loving-kindness, and understanding for ourselves and for others.

In Buddha's Eightfold Path—specifically, insight (or wisdom)—we reach the next point in how to find our purpose in life. To have wisdom means that we have an understanding that our behavior has consequences. Therefore, we want to have actions that will make us happy; in other words, whatever we do, we want to position ourselves to want peace and avoid suffering and not harm anyone.

Buddha taught that having right speech, right action, and right livelihood shapes our morality and conduct. Right speech deals with saying nothing that hurts others, and ourselves (self-criticism). Right action deals with having a peaceful and no-ill-intent behavior, with the intention of helping others also lead a more peaceful life.

Right livelihood means that whatever we do, in terms of profession or job or our goals, we must not bring harm to others (e.g., no cheating, lying, scheming, spying, backstabbing, or other destructive behavior). Discovering our life's purposes means that we can find them in the very actions we take.

Think about how you felt when you helped a friend solve a problem or when you brought joy to a family member who needed it. Happiness is in what you do and is in the very act of giving. Even the simplest actions can have a profound impact on someone. Saying *hello, thank you,* or *I'm sorry* can bring peace into someone's life.

There are times when it is best not to say anything at all. A good example of this is refraining from making a joke at someone else's expense. Your behavior—specifically, your actions (including speech)—can bring about feelings of joy to you and to others. Having right actions can align your life's purpose to happiness. And in turn, those same actions can give you direction to help you determine what your purpose in life is.

Goals

So far, we have discussed how your thoughts, insights, and behavior can shape your choice in your life's purpose. Our next topic is goals. It is important to have goals in life. Goals point our lives in a specific direction, like a compass helping us on our path of happiness. However, it's the journey that's important, not the desired result. If our minds are fixed on reaching a certain destination, then we will never stay in the present moment, and we will lose sight of all the things that matter.

A flagstick—the metal pole with a flag on it—is used in the game of golf to indicate the exact position of the hole on a green where a golfer must sink the ball. Try to view goals as signposts, not flagsticks; otherwise, wanting a specific outcome can create expectations that won't be fulfilled, and you will end up suffering for it.

Think of goals as a process in which you can connect to happiness. For example, if your goal is to become a millionaire, ask yourself how this goal can help you to connect to happiness. You could expand on your answer, as in the following: "In the process of becoming a millionaire, I will be mindful of my thoughts and actions. I will align my conduct and my business interactions to right speech, right action, and right livelihood. With mindful awareness, my goal is to connect to happiness and to avoid suffering in myself and others."

In the past, when I went fishing, my goal was always to catch a fish. As I got better, my goal changed to catching more fish. Many times, my goal of catching many fish did not come to fruition. In fact, many times I did not catch any fish at all. One day, I came home feeling disappointed, frustrated, and angered that I did not catch any fish. My wife saw how upset I was, and she asked me a simple question that had a profound effect on my thinking: "If fishing causes you to get so upset, why go fishing at all?"

She was right. My goal for fishing did not make me happy. It was not rooted in mindfulness, nor did it help me to live in and enjoy the present moment. I reflected on two questions: why do I go fishing, and which part of fishing do I enjoy? I soon realized that I needed to change my outlook, which meant that I needed to change my goal.

Today, I have several goals when I go fishing: stay in the present moment; enjoy everything and everyone around me; and if I catch a fish, be grateful. Of all the days that I have gone fishing, the most memorable one for me was a cold day in December with the snow falling. I saw a family of deer silently crossing the river. The beauty of that scene reached deep within my inner being and radiated a wonderous feeling of respect for nature and its wonders. When I returned home that day, I felt as if my spirit was renewed. To this day, I can't recall if I caught a fish that day.

Goals contribute to your life's purpose. Aligning them to mindfulness and proper behavior connects you to happiness.

Courage

In pursuing your life purpose, there can be moments when you get stuck. You might not be sure how to feel fulfilled or where to begin. You might be stuck in old patterns and habits. Maybe you have retired, but fear has prevented you from downsizing to an apartment that would allow you more time to travel. You justify your choice by saying, "Better to be safe than sorry." Maybe you feel that others have strong expectations of you that prevent you from pursuing your goals. If your parents wanted you to become a doctor, but your passion was creative writing, this expectation could seriously affect your pursuit of your life's purpose. Maybe you are unhappy in your job, but fear and family expectations have a hold on you, preventing you from looking for a new job or profession. Can you relate to the following statement? *I wish I had the courage to live my life free from fear, true to myself, and regardless of people's expectations.* Let's take a closer look at *fear* and *expectations*.

When we feel fear, we feel an unpleasant emotion, caused by a perceived threat of harm that comes from a physical or psychological danger. Danger is something that is real, but fear exists only in our thoughts. It can be unpleasant to deal with our fears. Even if the fear is unfounded, it can still *feel real* to us.

When we experience a specific fear, the unpleasantness of that feeling can bring anxiety (anxiety is synonymous with fear, but the perceived threat is anticipated versus immediate). When the brain stores these feared events, we then can become fearful of experiencing the unpleasantry. Think back to the first time you watched a scary movie. That night, when you went to bed, just the thought of the scary scenes in the movie might have re-created the fear again. The fear is unreal, but it still feels real.

Regardless of what type of fear is stopping or hindering us from pursuing our purposes in life, remember that we have tools (e.g., SAM meditation, relaxation meditation, mindfulness, self-compassion) that we can use to deal with fear. It takes great courage to deal with fear, and as such, we need lots of compassion and kindness toward ourselves.

Your goals and life purpose can be affected when people have expectations of you. The way that these expectations make you feel can determine your outlook on accepting or changing your goals and purpose in life. For example, your goal or purpose in life could be to become the president of the United States or to work as a political leader or activist in office. The people whom you serve would have many expectations of you. These expectations would shape and change your goals as you worked to satisfy these expectations. You would feel satisfied, rewarded, and even motivated by these expectations, and you would accept them as if they were part of your goals and life purpose.

On the other hand, you might feel that you need a new job or career, but you feel worried and are reluctant to change because of your partner's (or family's) expectations of you. Even if you got a new job, you might feel that these same expectations continued. As such, they would not encourage you to continue with your new goals and life purpose.

How you feel regarding people's expectations can affect your goals and life purpose. Start by asking yourself if you feel that there are expectations of you. Reflect on how they make you feel. Recognize your feelings and accept them with kindness toward yourself. It is important to be gentle with yourself to help you get through your feelings and prevent any self-blame and self-hatred (or hatred of any kind). Understand that it takes great courage to change or find your goals and purpose in life. The real you is the rose, living your life based on your opinion of yourself, devoid of someone else's expectation, standards, thinking, or belief.

To live your goals and your purpose in life is to live your life true to yourself. How you feel relative to others' expectations of you can affect your goals and life purpose, so take courage and be gentle with yourself.

Self-Doubt, Insecurities, Lack of Confidence

My experience has been that as we get older, our lack of confidence decreases but our insecurities increase. You might think that as you get older and the more experience you have, the less self-doubt you will have—but this is not the case. The reason for this is that as you age and experience more of the world, the world becomes smaller. You get to see all the unpredictable things that's in this world, and these things scare you. You experience the death a friend or family member through disease. You hear of all the troubles in the world. You talk to your family and friends and become aware of some of their problems and struggles. And all these things bring about fear, worry, and doubt. This, in turn, can create insecurities in you. With insecurities, you can easily question and analyze every possible decision you want to make.

Generally, I try not to listen to the evening news; I say to myself, *I have enough insecurities in my head already. I don't need to add more.* Whether we call it self-doubt, insecurities, or lack of confidence, they all point in a direction that can affect pursuing our goals and life purposes. I have the tools within myself to deal with fear, worry, and doubt. These tools can help me deal with my insecurities or my lack of confidence so that I can pursue changing goals and my life purpose. There was a point in my life when I wanted to learn more about mindfulness and meditation. I enrolled in a program that taught me the skills needed to become a mindfulness/meditation teacher.

After I completed the training program, a local yoga center asked me to teach mindfulness and meditation. Part of the teacher-training program required me to volunteer my time to teach the practice. After I completed the certification program, the same yoga center asked if I wanted to continue to teach mindfulness and meditation. At that time, I was not ready. I felt that I was still working through my own demons or my own insecurities, and I did not feel ready to teach anyone else.

When the global COVID-19 pandemic hit, my empathy became very strong for all people struggling through mental illness. This desire to help others inspired me to start teaching mindfulness and meditation. I reached out to the company for which I work and began teaching a virtual mindfulness/meditation program. Soon afterward, I put together several other training programs to help individuals deal with thoughts and strong emotions and to build a greater mental resilience. I was able to overcome my insecurities because of witnessing the struggles that others like me were going through.

But what do we do if we don't have an external stimulus

that is strong enough to help us to overcome our insecurities? That is difficult to answer because at times, our insecurities are there for a reason. Understanding why they are there can help bring mindful awareness so we can accept and work with these insecurities. When the student is ready, the teacher will appear—or when we accept and work with our insecurities, confidence can show up at our door and help us to get through them so that we can reach out to our goals and life purposes.

Sometimes it takes time; we need to work and feel comfortable with our insecurities before going to the next stage. Regardless of your insecurities, recognize them as part of who you are. If an insecurity is based on fear alone, simply recognize it and use the tools necessary to work with this fear. If the insecurities are strong, and you do not have the tools necessary to deal with them, reach out to someone who can help. Talk to a friend or a professional to give you some insight in understanding your insecurities. Make the effort to do what you can to educate yourself, and find resources that can help you to deal with insecurities.

There is one exception to the idea that as you get older, insecurities increase, That exception is my cat, Abby. When Abby was young, she was a lot more cautious and fearful about anything and anyone. As she got older, she gained more confidence in dealing with life and people around her. When Abby is with strangers, she relies on herself to know whom to trust and whom to stay away from. Her intuition guides her and overshadows any insecurities she might have. She knows what she wants, and she certainly expresses what she needs. She is a great role model for how to deal with insecurities. What advice would Abby give us regarding insecurities? I think she would say, "Live in the present moment, use your intuition (or awareness) to overcome your insecurities, and always be gentle with yourself."

Summary

To find our goals and life purposes, we must start within ourselves, looking for experiences that allow us to be happy. These experiences can help us find motivators to reach states of happiness, peace, and wholeness (or being complete). We are each unique, and we all have different goals and purposes in life. The question is, how do we find our goals and purposes in life? At the end of this chapter, is a "Finding Your Purpose in Life Guide," which summarizes the important concepts that help you find your goals and your life purpose.

Before closing this chapter, I want to echo a line from the movie *The Last Samurai*. Moritsugu Katsumoto is looking at a cherry blossom, and he says to Captain Nathan Algren, "The perfect blossom is a rare thing. You could spend your life looking for one, and it would not be a wasted life." At the end of the movie, Katsumoto says to Captain Algren, "All cherry blossoms are perfect."

As we go through life, we keep looking for that perfect thing that will make us happy. As Moritsugu Katsumoto found, however, every cherry blossom is perfect. Each cherry blossom is viewed uniquely by each person, as we all see beauty our own ways. If you spend your entire life enjoying the perfection of each cherry blossom in a state of peace, and you know that, at this very moment, you are complete and a spiritual being, yours will not have been a wasted life. The purpose of life is to connect to your happiness, moment by moment.

Finding Your Purpose in Life Guide

1. Be mindful of your thoughts, emotions, and feelings. Use awareness to help you see when you are responding, rather than reacting. By being mindful to your thoughts and actions, you can respond more clearly, which, in turn, can help guide you to find your goals and life purpose.
2. Drop all the demons. Drop all the things that are holding you back from finding your purpose and goals. When your intentions are free from attachments, frustration, disappointment, doubt, worry, blame, resentment, bitterness, anger, revenge, hatred, jealousy, guilt, or fear, you have removed all these barriers to happiness.
3. Recognize your rose. Recognize your gifts, no matter how big or small they are. See how you can use them to connect to happiness.
4. Look for the experiences in your life that have allowed you to connect to happiness. Reflect on these experiences, and ask yourself how they create meaning in

Finding Goals and a Life Purpose

your life; specifically, how they help you to connect to and feel happiness. See if you can incorporate these experiences into your goals and life purpose.

5. Align your goals and purpose in life to right speech, right action, and right livelihood. With mindful awareness and reflection, reevaluate your goals continuously to ensure they are rooted in happiness and to help avoid any suffering to yourself and others.

6. Reflect on fear. Ask yourself, "Do I have any fears regarding my goals or life's purpose? What am I afraid of? What do I fear the most?" List the fear(s), and list the different ways that you can work with your fear(s). Remember: Compassion! Compassion! Compassion!

7. Reflect on others' expectations of you that prevent you from pursuing your life's purpose. Ask yourself how these expectations make you feel. Recognize your feelings, and stay away from any self-criticism or self-hate (or hate of any kind). The real you is the rose, living your life based on your opinion of yourself and devoid of someone else's expectation, standards, thinking, or belief. To live your purpose in life and to reach your goals is to live your life true to yourself.

8. Do you have self-doubt or insecurities regarding what you want to do in life? Do you lack confidence? As Abby says, live in the present moment, use your intuition (or awareness) to overcome your insecurities, and always be gentle with yourself.

9. Remind yourself that the purpose of life is to connect to your happiness, moment by moment. If you spend your entire life enjoying the perfection of each cherry blossom, in a state of peace and knowing that, at this very moment, you are complete and a spiritual being, yours will not have been a wasted life.

CHAPTER ELEVEN

A Short Story— "The Enlightened Cat"

UP THE HIMALAYAS, A MOUNTAINOUS REGION IN ASIA, THERE lived a cat. This was no ordinary cat but a wise cat. The cat lived alone in a small cave, surrounded by lush greenery and with a small creek nearby. The area was very peaceful. After living alone for a long time, the cat decided to journey to the nearest town, which was three days away. The cat gathered her items for the journey and decided to leave the next day.

She awoke early in the morning to start her trip but noticed an angry sky. Seeing that it was going to rain, she decided to wait and see what the weather would bring. That day, as the rain fell, there was a cold wind, and the sky seemed to get angrier. She was cold in the cave, and so she built a fire for warmth. As she gazed into the fire, its flames produced a calming, hypnotic effect. She felt the heat on her fur and the light on her face, and she listened to the crackling sound of the fire.

The strong winds from the outside would occasionally reach the fire and make it grow stronger. She felt the cold chill from the wind but also felt the heat rise from the fire. As the sound of the rain began to quiet down, she closed her eyes and listened to all the sounds. At first, she listened to the fire, then she moved to the sounds of the wind, then the rain, and finally, she focused her attention beyond them all.

In the distance, she heard the trees rustling against each other. Branches were fighting against each other, the occasional battle ending with the drop of a branch to the ground. Then, without warning, there was a large flash of light, followed by a thunderclap. The wise cat was startled at first, but she continued to focus her attention, listening beyond each sound. From the trees, she heard nothing; she paused for a while in the silence.

The fire began to die down, and the cold kept coming. She got up and reached for another piece of wood. Sparks and smoke rose from the fire as she placed the wood onto the fire. One of the sparks seemed to have a life of its own as it traveled up into the air and danced away with the wind. The wise cat noticed this and simply observed.

The wind calmed down, and the rain started to slow down. At a distance, a faint shimmer of light started to peek out from the clouds. The cat got up. She gathered some herbs that were drying at the far end of the cave. A pawful of herbs was enough to make some tea. Carefully, she assembled the tripod to hold the kettle over the fire to start the process. She paused for a moment but then went back to adjust the kettle's height so that the bottom of the kettle was at the top of the flames.

Before adding the herbs, she leaned over to smell them. The scents of chamomile and peppermint were very pleasing and relaxing. She added them to the boiling water and watched as the aroma infused the surrounding air. The rain stopped, and the wind died down completely. The small crack of light in the clouds slowly began to open. She walked over to the entrance of the cave and stared into the clouds.

"Those beautiful clouds have lessened to a single word called *cloud*," she said to herself. She returned to the boiling kettle and carefully inserted the ladle to scoop up a cup of tea. The cup that she used was a simple cup. She was fond of it but had no expectations of it. Slowly, she sipped the tea and felt the warmth from the cup as she pressed it upon her chest. The peppermint was just a bit stronger than the chamomile. Silence was now in the air.

She doused the fire. *No time like the present*, she thought as she picked up her things and left the cave. The sun was out, and the cold air grew warmer. In her backpack, she had placed some food, her kettle, the ladle, the cup, herbs, a wool blanket, and her journal.

She took her walking stick and cloak, which her teacher had given her. "A stick to ground you," the teacher had always said. She had asked him to explain the meaning of the cloak. He had answered, "To keep the rain off your head. What else?"

She walked slowly, as the area was still wet from the fallen rain. When her mind drifted, she returned it to the walking stick. The feeling of that old stick was comforting. It was a stick to check the depth of water, to push away the tall grass, to keep her upright and balanced. When her mind drifted, she felt the grip and listened to the sound it made with each touch to the ground. Down the path she went, through the tall grass, until she came along the edge of the creek.

The creek was flowing high and muddy. Crossing at that point was not safe. Eventually, the creek would settle of its own accord. She followed the creek for several hours until she came upon the master tree, where she stopped to take a break. She sat down and leaned against the tree. Many times, she had come to this tree. She had used very small pieces of its bark in tea to help with headaches and fever. She closed her eyes and felt its presence. Its leaves and branches moved with the wind, but its trunk was deep in stillness.

She opened her eyes and realized that she had dozed off, probably for an hour or two. She took a long stretch and started off again. Turning back to the master tree, she bowed down and graciously said thank you.

The clouds and cold wind returned. She continued following the creek. Up ahead was a rocky area of the creek that was wide but shallow and easy to cross. Just on the other side and a bit downstream was a small holding pool for fish. She reached the crossing area; by now, the water level had dropped. With her walking stick making its way, she followed slowly. The water was still somewhat discolored, but the water was shallow in this part so it was easy to see the bottom. One step at a time, she reached the other side and rested for a minute, taking a few slow, deep breaths. Moving downstream again, she followed the creek to the holding pool. *Just in time for an early dinner*, she thought. Her favorite fishing spot was on top of a rock at the edge of this pool. The small bait fish would hide around this rock. She poised herself on the rock and waited—one mind with focus on any movement in the water. It didn't take long to catch dinner. A few fish were all she needed.

The sun was out again. She reached into her backpack and pulled out her wool blanket. She found a small hilltop and placed the blanket on the ground. She sat on the blanket and closed her eyes. At first, just like the creek, her thoughts rushed by, fast and unclear. She kept watching her thoughts, and in time, they began to slow down. Now she was able to see each thought, one by one. Without any judgment, she just watched. A couple of times, a thought would grab her attention. When she noticed this, she simply returned as the watcher.

Time passed, and she shifted her attention to her breath. She took several deep breaths, slowly in and out, while noticing any feelings or emotions. She shifted her attention to belly breathing. She placed one paw on her belly to help her feel the movement and to slow down the breath. The sounds of birds, the wind, and the creek were there, but her focus was on the breath. When she was done with her meditation, she wished herself to be happy and to avoid suffering and the causes of suffering. She wished the same for all other sentient beings.

She packed up all her belongings and made her way downstream again. She decided that since the fishing was good, she would keep with the creek and try to take advantage of another meal. The terrain changed slightly to open grounds. The view was astonishing, revealing the forest in the distance, the rocky shelf at the far right, and every flower imaginable in between. Slowly, she hiked through the open ground, absorbing the beauty of it all. It took a couple of hours to reach the forest.

She found a cherry blossom and decided that this tree would make a good spot for camp. She headed for the creek. The water was a bit deeper in this area, but she still managed to find a meal. When she was done, she used her kettle to bring back some water and gathered some twigs to start a fire. Using her flint and metal striker, she produced a fire and placed her kettle at the edge of it. After making herself comfortable, she pulled out her journal from her backpack.

The journal was a gift from her teacher for her first birthday. She skimmed through her notes, and near the back she found this line: "Use these tools to help you find the key that is within yourself, to a better you, free from suffering, and to a path of enlightenment." She spent some time in reflecting on those words.

The tea was ready; using her ladle, she scooped up some tea from the kettle and poured it carefully into her cup. After placing the ladle down, she slowly enjoyed every drop of tea. The day was at its end, and it was time for sleep. She gripped her wool blanket and made up a bed in the blossom tree, finding find a safe and comfortable spot. With her blanket and cloak nestled together, she dozed off to sleep. The ambers slowly died off, and the wind that night was calm.

She awoke early in the morning and began with meditation, as she found her mind tended to be calmer before starting the day. Concentrative practice was what she liked to do, giving sustained attention to breathing. This type of meditation helped her with focus, especially when her mind seemed unsettled, as it did today—she was out of her regular routine with this journey to town, not to mention sleeping all night in a tree.

Her teacher would say, "A mind is like the weather—rain one day, sunshine the next. Simply observe, and it will pass." She made one more trip to the creek before heading off again. The next part of the journey was through the forest, which would take about a day. She entered the forest, bringing only awareness into it. *Bring fear, and you get fear,* she thought. The sun was out, and the forest was warm and welcoming. She spent several hours easily walking through the forest, as the ground was flat with a mild slope downward.

In the distance was a small opening, devoid of any trees, which allowed the full strength of the sun to penetrate. She rested there, feeling the warmth of the sun. Her mind drifted, and she thought about her family and wondered how each one was doing. Her thoughts moved toward worry and despair. She repeated the word *worry* several times to distance herself from these thoughts. Then, she closed her eyes and imagined a white light filled with blessings. She whispered, "May you be blessed and filled with positive energy." She repeated these words as she sent the white light to each member of her family.

The rest of the day, she continued walking to reach the edge of the forest before nightfall. At the edge, she would have better luck finding something to eat, as prey would scurry along the ground, in and out of the forest in the dark of night. Hours passed, and her tummy began to rumble. It would be another hour or two before the sun would set.

Her body began to ache, as her muscles were not accustomed to the continuous travel. Finally, she reached the edge. She dared not risk lighting a fire here, which might start a larger and uncontrollable fire. A fire also might scare any small prey in the area. She found a tree to settle against and rested for a while. Nightfall came, and she slowly made her way to spot where she would wait in darkness. Hunting at night was a skill that she knew very well. Once in a while, fear would creep in, but her focus on what she was doing kept it at bay.

Success! The hunt was now over. *Death cannot be avoided*, she thought. She went back to the tree to settle for the night. She grabbed her backpack and climbed up the tree to find a safe spot, away from the larger prey that also prowled at night. Both her cloak and wool blanket were dark in color, which concealed her at night. She curled into them and soon was asleep.

Before the sun rose, a curious owl landed in the same tree near her. She opened her eyes, only to find two more looking at her. Her instinct recognized that the owl was not a threat, only curious. The owl studied her and eventually flew away. She relied on her instinct instead of reacting out of fear. If fear should take over, she had the tools to work with it. "Far easier to accept the current instead of fighting against it," her teacher would say.

A Short Story—"The Enlightened Cat"

She climbed down the tree and decided to leave the forest. The next part of the journey would be a bit more difficult, as the area was somewhat rocky and open to the weather. *There will be no accommodations here,* she thought. The walking stick proved very useful in this terrain, as balance was necessary to keep from injury.

The sun started to peek out, but the clouds were on their way. By midmorning, the clouds covered the sky, and rain began forming. She covered her head with the cloak's hood and stopped occasionally to listen to the rain. She was taught that direct attention to an external sound can help calm the mind and provide focus. The wind picked up, bringing with it darker clouds and heavier rain. She moved a bit slower but steadily.

She took advantage of the little pools of water that formed by drinking from them. She saw fresh herbs growing between a few bushes and decided to gather some for a light snack for later. *I guess I was wrong. There are accommodations here. I shouldn't judge,* she thought.

The rain continued all day. By evening, she finally reached the path, which was more of a narrow trail. When she looked carefully, she could see the tramping of footprints, which slowed the growth of grass. The cat figured that another half-day walk on the path would get her to the town. Once again, she looked for a tree where she could spend the night. She looked for a thicker and denser tree to provide comfort from the rain.

Once up in the tree, she found her spot to settle. Resting now, she closed her eyes and said, "I am not my thoughts. My thoughts are not who I am. I accept my thoughts nonjudgmentally and allow them to pass. I am not my emotions. My emotions are not who I am. They pass through me like the changing weather. My fears, worries, and doubts are not true. I accept them, notice them, and allow them to pass through. I watch my thoughts now and observe without any reaction. I watch my thoughts now. I watch my thoughts now. I focus on my breath now and concentrate on its movement. I focus on my breath; I see it enter my nose, down into my lungs, and out again. I focus on my breath now. I focus on my breath now." Shortly afterward, she fell asleep.

The sun was out early. She opened her eyes and gave thanks for a wonderful moment. She focused her attention on the area of her heart and brought her teacher to her mind; he had brought so much love, joy, and forgiveness into her world. She thought about how much support he gave, how much he cared for her. She stayed with this feeling and breathed it in. Finally, exhaled and allowed the feeling to grow outward. She said aloud, "May others feel gratitude."

She climbed down from the tree and started on the path. It was a pleasant walk, as the sun warmed her body after the dampness of the night. From the corner of her eye, she noticed a flower that had lost some of its petals. Her mind drifted back to when she first met her teacher. That first day, he had taught her about blame and that it creates suffering. He had said, "Remember this to help you get through blame: when you look to nature, the flower does not blame the wind for losing its petals; instead, the petals simply fall."

She was excited that she would see him soon. She returned

her attention to the walking stick, as it grounded her to the present moment.

The town was now in view. She could see the streets, the people, and, of course, the food. Outside vendors were selling their products and the day's catch. She could faintly smell bread baking from one of the houses in the distance. *How wonderful*, she thought. She carefully entered the town so as not to draw any attention.

The town was simple in the sense that it had a few places to eat and drink, several small stores, and two places to stay overnight. In the middle of the town was a temple. She went inside and saw several people praying and a few meditating. The scent of candles and sweet-smelling incense filled the air. The right side of the temple was lined with pictures and statues, while the left side had different teachings hanging along the wall. As she walked slowly to the back of the temple, she studied all the sights around her. She left the temple through a back door that entered a garden. This garden was filled with flowers, carefully trimmed bushes, and several large trees. Placed throughout the garden were several areas where she could sit and enjoy the moment. The same creek that was near her home flowed along the side of this garden. Across the creek on the other side was the monastery. She made her way to a wooden bridge that crossed over the creek and into the entryway of the monastery. She was back!

The door to the monastery opened, and Sister Abigail came out to greet her with a warm hug. "It has been many years since I last saw you, and I feel as if you only left yesterday. It is wonderful that you are back. Come. I am sure you are hungry and thirsty. Let us eat together and enjoy our time together." They made their way to the kitchen, and Sister Abigail prepared a meal and some tea. They spoke for several hours, discussing their lives in terms of happiness, joy, peace, and suffering.

The afternoon temple bells rang, and, without hesitation, they both stopped, closed their eyes, and took several slow, deep breaths. The ringing of the bells invited all who heard them to pause and be present in the moment.

"Stay as long as you want. I'm sure you remember where your old room is. Now, I must go to the temple and lead the afternoon meditation session. Peace be with you, my young daughter." Sister Abigail left for the temple, and the wise cat headed to her old room.

She dropped her backpack on the table near the bed and left the walking stick behind the door. The window in the room overlooked the garden. She opened the window slightly and could hear the calming sounds of water running from the creek. She decided to rest so she climbed into bed. Her eyes began to close slowly, as old thoughts drifted through her mind. Soon, she fell asleep with the sound of the creek carrying those memories.

She heard a knock on the door. Sister Abigail had come by to bring her some towels and an extra blanket. The wise cat asked Sister if the teacher was available.

"He is coming back late this evening, as he is visiting a dying friend. Tomorrow morning would be a good time to see him. For now, rest and then join us later for dinner and evening meditation. I brought you a new journal, as I am sure you will have some questions for your teacher," said Sister Abigail.

The wise cat thanked her and bowed repeatedly as the sister left her room. She examined the journal and felt every inch of the book. She sat down at the table and began to write:

> When I close my eyes, I watch my mind. As my mind generates thoughts, I try to become aware that a thought has been generated. Because my mind is limitless, any thought is possible. I try not to judge any thought that comes in. I observe it without feeding any energy to it. If my thoughts come too fast, I say, "It's OK," and I observe, just like watching a river after a rain. If I become agitated or frustrated, I take a couple of slow, deep breaths and focus my attention on the breath. I realize that I have absolutely no control over the thoughts that come into my mind. I practice routinely and notice that, with time, it becomes easier.

She closed the journal and got cleaned up before going on with the rest of the day. The warm water was comforting, and it felt great to freshen up. From the window, she could see Sister Abigail attending to the garden. The cat made her way down to the garden; she wanted to assist the sister with any necessary chores. She recalled her teacher saying, "Chores are opportunities to practice maintaining focus on the task at hand. They are essentially a way to exercise meditation in the activity itself to help with concentration. When the mind is on the task, there is no past, future, or storyline, only one mind."

They spent the rest of the afternoon until dinner working together in the garden and enjoying each other's company. They prepared dinner together, and at one point, the wise cat turned to Sister Abigail and said, "When you live in a cave, you can easily forget the enjoyment of others."

Sister Abigail responded, "Why did you leave?"

The wise cat paused for a while and then answered, "I felt that I needed to work on myself. After my mother died, I had a hard time dealing with my feelings. I seemed to lose—or at least to question—my purpose in life. It is difficult to be in service to others when you are not there. I like helping others, but I needed some alone time to regain my balance. Both you and the teacher were very helpful during this time, and I will always be grateful for your help. It was the teacher who suggested that I take a three-day journey into the mountains. He also gave me directions to the cave and suggested that I journal my thoughts and feelings to make room for healing.

"When I reached the cave, days turned into months, and months turned into years. Then one day, I was walking along the creek, and I saw a mother deer and her fawn. Suddenly, I began weeping. I wept and wept until no more tears came out. Then, the whole world just stopped, and my mind suddenly became clear, as if a fog had lifted. I could smell everything around me, and I could hear all the sounds. I felt a profound

A Short Story—"The Enlightened Cat"

sense of peace. Days passed, and I felt connected to my inner happiness. That is what brought me back here."

The sister reached over to the cat and gave her a long hug.

After dinner, they both walked to the temple to join the evening meditation. Sister Abigail introduced with wise cat to Brother Jack Russell (called Brother Jacky, for short), who was leading the meditation session. Brother Jacky was a therapist who worked with people who needed help with strong emotions and matters of the heart. Many people traveled far just to speak to him. Not only was he knowledgeable, but he had a big heart and a very calm demeanor. Sister Abigail joked in front of Brother Jacky, saying, "If there was a fire, you, Brother Jacky, would take your time to leave the burning building."

They all laughed together. Then the temple bells rang to signify that the meditation session would begin shortly. They all went inside the temple, and Brother Jacky went to the front to begin the guided meditation. There was a deep silence in the temple now.

Brother Jacky closed his eyes; a half smile was on his face as he spoke in a soothing voice. "Welcome and thank you, everyone, for coming tonight. I invite you to pick a posture or position that makes you feel comfortable. If you find it painful or uncomfortable to sit, you can lie on the floor or sit in a chair. Let's start by taking a couple of deep breaths—slowly in, slowly out. Notice your breath in this moment. Is there anything going on in your life? How do you feel? To deny our emotions, fears, and worries is to deny ourselves from moving forward in our lives.

"Feel any senses in the body that arises. Take a couple of minutes to scan from the top of your head to the bottom of your feet for any senses. Remember that there is no right or wrong way of doing this. Sense any emotions that are present. Where do you feel these emotions in your body? If you can't feel anything, then simply focus your attention on the breath. If you do feel an emotion, explore it from a distance nonjudgmentally. If it helps, try breathing into the emotion. Let's try this for a couple of minutes.

"Next comes loving-kindness and self-compassion. We need them when we are suffering. We need loving-kindness and compassion toward ourselves to help us get through these moments by preventing any self-blame and self-hatred. Cultivate loving-kindness and self-compassion. Visualize someone in your mind who is very compassionate. See that person sending you kindness and compassion. If it helps, you can see this as white light being sent from the person to you. Now, embrace the kindness and compassion, and breathe into it. Let's spend some time feeling this positive energy."

When the meditation session was done, everyone left the temple except for Sister Abigail and the wise cat, who stayed behind for some quiet evening prayers to end the day.

The next morning, the wise cat got up early to do her meditation. When she was finished, she opened her journal and began writing.

A Short Story—"The Enlightened Cat"

Dear Journal,

I feel complete. I feel at peace in this moment. Thoughts and emotions come and go, but they do not disturb me as before. I want to stay here at the monastery, but first I must speak to the teacher to get his guidance and blessing. I want to continue learning and gaining wisdom here. I also want to help others. I think I can learn a lot from Brother Jacky. He would be a great teacher for me. I especially want to deepen my meditation practice. The connection to the people, the temple, the garden, and the creek is what I enjoy the most.

She closed the journal and took several deep breaths; then she reminded herself not to have any expectations. Feeling grounded, she made her way to see the teacher.

The teacher lived at the far end of the monastery, just past the library. The wise cat poked her head into the library to see if anything had changed. In the center of the library was a sitting area with a few desks. The library also had a large private room used as a teaching center. There were many types of books, but most were centered on well-being. She reflected on the many teachings she had received from the teacher when she was a student. With a smile, she left the library.

The door leading to the teacher's room had a note on it addressed to her. She opened the note, and it read, "I'm at the creek." She knew right away that he was at his favorite spot. He usually went there once a week to immerse himself in deep reflection. It was about fifteen minutes just outside of town. She went back to her room to get her walking stick and cloak before proceeding with this short hike. Instead of walking back through the town, she took a bit of a longer path by following the creek downstream from the garden to where the teacher was. That area of the creek had a small waterfall. He said he liked going there just to listen to the waterfall.

The teacher was sitting on the grass under a tree. As she approached him, he opened his eyes and looked up at her. He stood up and gave her a long, warm hug. He said to her, "I remember when you used to follow me here, thinking that I would not see you. But I always knew when you were here. It never took long before I could hear you chasing the fish up the creek. It was a sound that I always enjoyed hearing. Now, please sit and tell me what is on your mind."

The wise cat said, "I'm sorry to hear about your friend. Sister Abigail mentioned that you were with him yesterday. How is he doing?"

The teacher paused for a moment before saying, "He is very weak but in good spirits. I have been working with him how to *stay* with the pain. We've known each other since we were children. He too has been a great teacher to me. Whenever I thought I'd lost my ego, he was always the one to find it. Anyway, enough of me and my old friend. Please tell me about you."

The wise cat answered, "I wish to return and stay at the monastery. When I left, there was a void in my heart. I have found that this was not an empty void but only feelings that I'd pushed away—feelings that I did not want to bring to light. I blamed myself for my mom's accident. If I had been home that day, maybe there would not have been a fire, or I could have saved her. It took me a long time to realize that when the petals fall, the flower does not blame the wind. It is as *it is* and nothing more. It took my suffering to bring light into the shadow of my heart. I wept hard one day when I remembered my mom, and that was the turning point in my suffering. I acknowledged my feelings and was no longer ashamed of them. I accepted them all and resisted none.

"This process took a long time, but when I started to accept kindness and compassion for myself, that helped my healing. I felt the transformation from suffering to healing. A deep sense of peace filled me. I spent several days in this bliss, and I simply observed. Then, my heart spoke to me, and I heard the calling back to the monastery. I felt like a cup of tea filled to the rim, and I wanted to share what I had with others. I learned from the struggles that I went through, and all that you and Sister Abigail taught me fell into place. I felt that I could use this source to help others in their struggles with pain and suffering. But that is not all that I felt. You and Sister Abigail are not only my teachers; you are my family."

The teacher got up and asked the wise cat to follow him. He led her to the waterfall and said, "The water always returns to its source, where it started. It may be the rain, the dew, the underground spring, or the creek, but it always ends up being water, no matter the form. You are the water. Yesterday, you were the rain, and today, you are the creek, but deep within you, you are still the water, and that never changes. I am glad you have found that peace that was always inside you. And I am glad that you have decided to stay." The teacher turned around and started walking.

The wise cat followed him and asked, "Where are we going?"

He replied, "I'm hungry. Let's go home and get some breakfast."

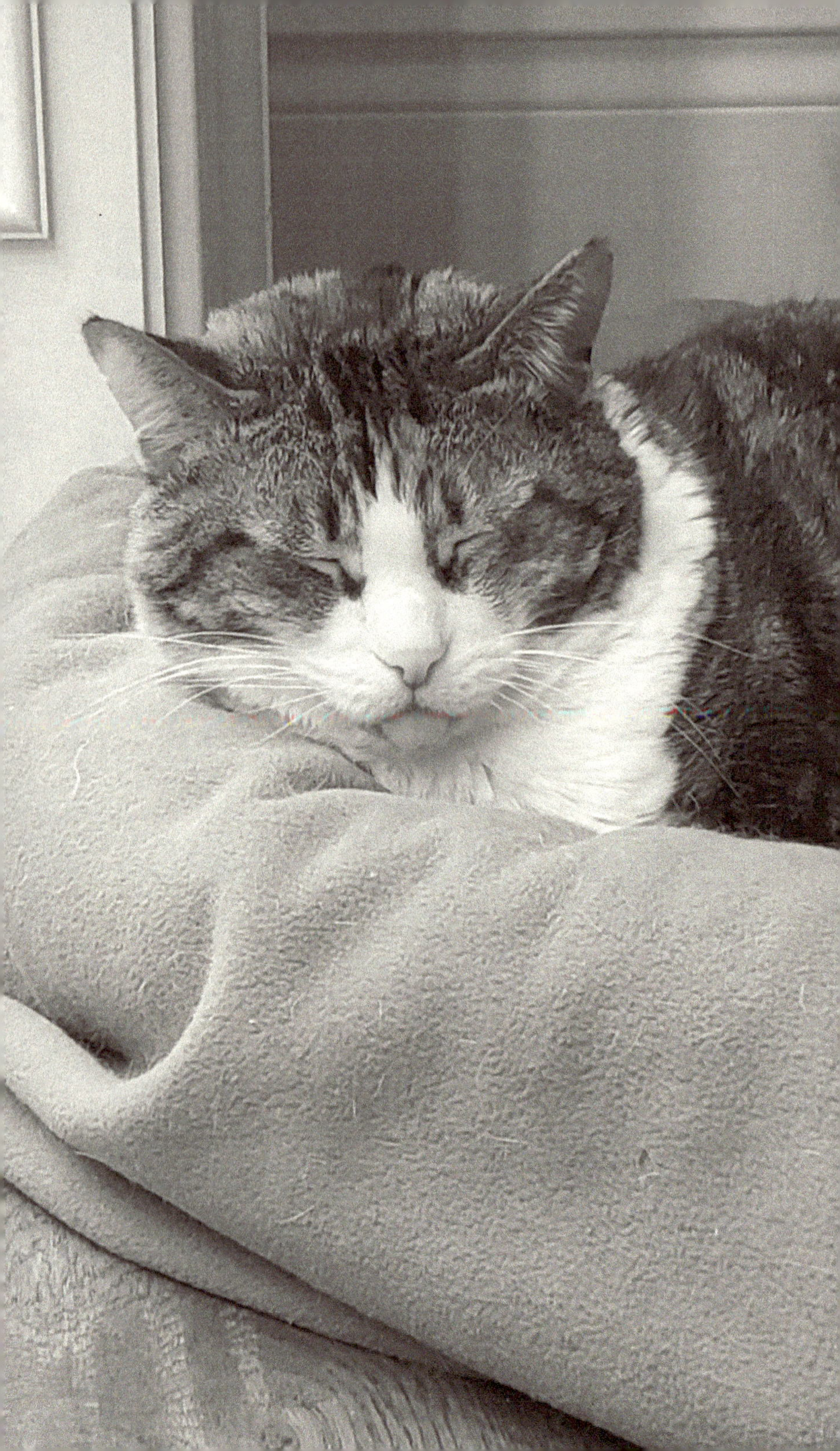

CLOSING MEOWS

I HOPE THAT YOU HAVE FOUND PRACTICAL AND WORKABLE SOLUTIONS to help you connect to happiness. I can only remind you that the key is daily practice in mindfulness, meditation, self-compassion, and loving-kindness. In time, with habitual practice, your brain's neuronal connections will change, and new thought processes will be laid to ultimately help you deal with suffering and bring you back to your inner peace. As your mind becomes quieter and calmer, you will have a greater ability to connect to happiness. Use these skills to continuously guide your thoughts, speech, and actions. May you be filled with happiness, and may you be the light for others to see.

> Happiness is being in a state of peace and knowing that, at this very moment, you are complete and a *beautiful* spiritual being.

God bless, and namaste.

CPSIA information can be obtained
at www.ICGtesting.com
Printed in the USA
BVHW081138060522
636177BV00001B/8